30knit PONCHOS & CAPES

Rita Maassen

STACKPOLE BOOKS
Guilford, Connecticut

Published by Stackpole Books
An imprint of The Rowman & Littlefield Publishing Group, Inc.
4501 Forbes Blvd., Ste. 200
Lanham, MD 20706
www.stackpolebooks.com

Distributed by NATIONAL BOOK NETWORK
800-462-6420

The original German edition was published as *Ponchos und Capes stricken*.
Copyright © 2016 frechverlag GmbH, Stuttgart, Germany (www.frech.de)
This edition is published by arrangement with Claudia Böhme Rights & Literary Agency,
Hannover, Germany (www.agency-boehme.com)

2019 English translation published by Stackpole Books

Photography: frechverlag GmbH, 70499 Stuttgart; lichtpunkt, Michael Ruder, Stuttgart
Product management: Franziska Schmidt
Editing: Regina Sidabras, Berlin
Series design: Katrin Röhlig
Typesetting: Petra Theilfarth
Translation: Katharina Sokiran

We have made every effort to ensure the accuracy and completeness of these instructions. We
cannot, however, be responsible for human error, typographical mistakes, or variations in individual work.

British Library Cataloguing in Publication Information available

Library of Congress Cataloging-in-Publication Data

Names: Maassen, Rita, author.
Title: 30 knit ponchos and capes / Rita Maassen.
Other titles: Ponchos und Capes stricken. English | Thirty knit ponchos and
  capes
Description: Guilford, Connecticut : Stackpole, [2019] | Translation of:
  Ponchos und Capes stricken. Stuttgart, Germany : Frechverlag GmbH, 2016.
Identifiers: LCCN 2018033844 | ISBN 9780811737098 (pbk. : alk. paper)
Subjects: LCSH: Knitting—Patterns. | Ponchos. | Cloaks.
Classification: LCC TT825 .M1313 2019 | DDC 746.43/2—dc23 LC record available at https://lccn.
loc.gov/2018033844

♾™ The paper used in this publication meets the minimum requirements of American National
Standard for Information Sciences—Permanence of Paper for Printed Library Materials, ANSI/
NISO Z39.48-1992.

Printed in the United States of America

APRIL 2019

30knit PONCHOS & CAPES

Easy-to-wear styles
for any occasion

CONTENTS

INTRODUCTION

Ponchos and capes are absolute must-haves! These basics shouldn't be missing from any closet, including yours! The great thing about these wonderful throw-on pieces is that, in addition to being fashionable and trendy, they can go with every style and will complement any outfit.

In this book, you will find patterns for a variety of different ponchos and capes. Whether cozily warm or light and airy, long or short, with sleeves, buttoned or closed, hooded, or even with a matching cowl, you are sure to find your favorite one! Featuring lace patterns, colorwork designs, or cables, every knitted piece is something special.

Thanks to three difficulty levels, this book contains something for everyone, from beginner to experienced knitter. A short section about knitting basics starting on page 92 explains the most important techniques in a simple and easy-to-understand way.

Grab your knitting needles and get started.

Patterns are rated in difficulty levels:
- ●○○   quick and easy
- ●●○   more time-consuming
- ●●●   for experienced knitters

PONCHOS

LEANA

Square, stylish, beautiful

STOCKINETTE STITCH
In rows: Knit on RS, purl on WS.
In rounds: Knit all sts in all rounds.

RIBBING PATTERN 1
Alternate knit 2, purl 2.

RIBBING PATTERN 2
Alternate purl 2, knit 2.

Instructions

BACK
With DPN set and C, CO 8 sts and evenly
distribute onto DPNs. Join into round
and knit 1 rnd, marking beginning of
round with a piece of contrasting color
yarn. Place a removable marker directly
onto each of sts #2, 4, 6, and 8.
Work Rnd 2 as follows: *K1, M1R, k1, M1L,
repeat from * 3 times more—16 sts.
Rnd 3: Knit all sts.
Rnd 4: *Knit to next marked st, M1R, knit
the marked st, M1L, repeat from * 3 times
more—8 sts increased, 24 total sts.
Rnd 5: Knit all sts.
Repeat Rnds 4 and 5 all the time. When
needles become crowded, change to
short circular needle and, depending on
stitch count, later to next longer circular.
After 30 rnds from CO, you will have 120 sts
on the needles. Proceed in the following
stripe sequence, continuing to work
increases up to the next-to-last rnd, until
you have 384 sts on the needles: *2 rnds

B, 2 rnds C, rep from * 2 times more, 22
rnds B, **2 rnds A, 2 rnds B, rep from **
2 times more, 22 rnds A—384 sts.
In the next rd, work as follows: BO 96 sts
and break working yarn, leaving a long
tail; transfer the following 96 sts to the
first, then the next 96 sts to the second
spare needle to hold. Over the remaining
96 sts, work in back-and-forth rows with
turning on circular needle. For the left-
side panel, work 40 rows in Stockinette
and 8 rows in Ribbing patt 1, then BO all
sts. For the right-side panel, work in A
over the 96 sts from the first spare needle: 40 rows Stockinette and 8 rows in
Ribbing patt 2, then BO all sts.
Rotate work so that the sts held on the
second spare needle are at the top. Now,
with circular knitting needle, pick up and
knit 38 sts from the side edge of the
left-side panel (including ribbed edging),
transfer the 96 formerly held sts from the
second spare needle to the circular needle, too, and from the side edge of the
right side panel, again pick up and knit
38 sts—172 sts. Work 8 rows in Ribbing
patt, then BO all sts.

FRONT
Work the same as the Back, but with neckline shaping. For this, after 84 rnds from
CO (= 8 rnds in A, or when there are 336
sts on the needles), continue as follows:
k29, BO 26 sts, k281. Break yarn, leaving a
long tail, and distribute the sts on the

SIZE

One size = S–XXL
48 in x 32 in (120 cm x 80 cm)

MATERIALS

#4 medium-weight yarn in 3 colors;
shown in Schoppel Alpaka Queen;
50% wool, 50% alpaca; 219 yd (200
m), 3.5 oz (100 g) per skein; A: #9755
Grey-Heathered Anthracite, 17.6 oz
(500 g), B: #9680 Grey, 7 oz (200 g),
and C: #9220 Light Grey Heathered,
3.5 oz (100 g)

US 8 (5.0 mm) circular needles, in
lengths 24 in (60 cm), 32 in (80 cm),
and 48 in (120 cm)

US 6 (4.0 mm) set of DPNs

4 removable stitch markers

2 spare needles

GAUGE

Stockinette st on US 8 (5.0 mm)
needles, 18 sts and 24 rows = 4 in x
4 in (10 cm x 10 cm)

circular needle so that both needle tips exit at the neck opening (to the right and left of the bound-off 26 sts) and face each other. From here on, continue in A in rows: For neckline shaping, at the inner (neckside) edge, BO sts on both sides in every other row as follows: 4 sts once, 3 sts once, 2 sts once, and 1 st twice. At the same time, continue increases at the marked sts in every RS row as before. When neck opening has reached a height of 12 rows, continue as follows: BO the first 24 sts, and break working yarn, leaving a long tail. Transfer next 96 sts to first spare needle and following 96 sts to second spare needle for holding. Now, k96, and BO the last 24 sts. Break yarn, leaving a long tail. Work side panels and bottom ribbing the same as for the Back. Work Ribbing patt on side panels mirror-inverted—that is, for left side panel, work 8 rows in Ribbing patt 2, and for right side panel, 8 rows in Ribbing patt 1.

FINISHING

Soak pieces in lukewarm water and carefully press out excess water. Spread out on a soft surface, block to measurements, and let dry.

Close shoulder seams.

With DPNs, pick up and knit 116 sts around neckline edge, evenly distribute onto DPNs, and continue in rnds. Place marker for beginning of round and work 12 rnds in Ribbing patt. BO all sts and weave in ends.

MAJA

Houndstooth check

SEED STITCH FOR EVEN STITCH COUNT

In RS rows: Alternate k1, p1.
In WS rows: Alternate p1, k1.

SEED STITCH FOR ODD STITCH COUNT

In RS and WS rows: Alternate k1, p1, ending with k1.

HOUNDSTOOTH PATTERN

Row 1 (B): K1, *slip 1 st purlwise, k2, rep from * all the time, ending with slip 1 st purlwise, k1.
Row 2 (B): Purl all sts.
Row 3 (A): *Slip 1 st purlwise, k2, rep from * all the time.
Row 4 (A): Purl all sts.
Repeat Rows 1–4 all the time.

SIZE

One size = S–XXL
Rectangles: 20 in x 37½ in (50 cm x 95 cm)

Size US 6 (4.0 mm) circular needle, 24 in (60 cm) long

8 brown marbled wooden buttons, approx. ¾ in (18 mm)

MATERIALS

#3 light-weight yarn in 2 colors; shown in Schoppel On Touch; 100% superwash merino wool; 137 yd (125 m), 1.75 oz (50 g) per skein; A: #5011 Light Blue, 8.8 oz (250 g), and B: #7640 Hazelnut, 14.1 oz (400 g)

GAUGE

In Houndstooth patt with US 6 (4.0 mm) needles, 23 sts and 36 rows = 4 in x 4 in (10 cm x 10 cm)

Instructions

FIRST HALF OF PONCHO

With B, CO 117 sts and, for the edging, work 10 rows in Seed st. In the last row k2tog the 1st and 2nd st—116 sts.

Now, continue in the following pattern sequence: 7 sts Seed st in B, 102 sts Houndstooth patt, 7 sts Seed st in B, working from a separate ball.

After 322 rows in this Houndstooth patt, work another 10 rows in Seed st in B over all sts, making an M1R increase in Row 1 after the first st—117 sts. BO all sts.

SECOND HALF OF PONCHO

Work as first half, but with buttonholes and without Seed st edging at the top. For this, after 6 rows from CO, in a RS row, at the right edge, work the first buttonhole as follows: 2 sts in Seed st, BO 2 sts, continue in pattern sequence to end of row. In the next WS row, over the 2 bound-off sts, CO 2 new sts and incorporate them into the stitch pattern. Make 7 more buttonholes in this manner in every 25th row. After this, continue as described for the first half of the poncho, but BO all sts after having worked 322 rows in Houndstooth patt.

FINISHING

Soak the two rectangles in lukewarm water, carefully press out excess water, and spread them out on a soft surface to block. Let pieces dry, then sew both halves together as follows: Place the first poncho half (the one without buttonholes), RS facing up, on the floor, with narrow sides at top and bottom. Now, position second half, also RS facing up, horizontally at bottom right to first half, with buttonholes at the top and narrow side without Seed st band at left (see schematic). Sew both pieces together at the adjoining edges. Now, rotate the narrow side of the first half clockwise until it completely touches the bottom part of the second half. Place the buttonhole band above the Seed stitch band of the first half and mark button placement with tailor pins. Sew buttons to first half of poncho in marked spots.

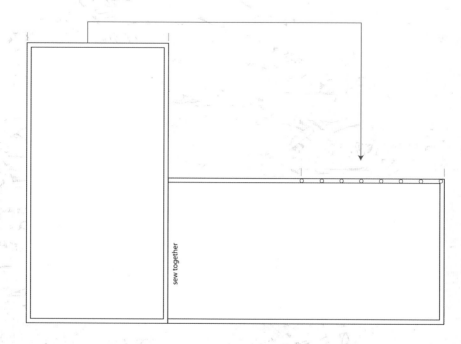

sew together

MARIANA

Color pattern pizzazz

STOCKINETTE STITCH

In rounds: Knit all sts in all rounds.

GARTER STITCH

In rounds: Alternate one round of all knit sts with one round of all purl sts.

COLORWORK PATTERN

Work all rnds in Stockinette according to Colorwork Chart. Repeat the pattern repeat (12 sts wide) widthwise, ending with the st after the pattern repeat. Work Rnds 1–44 a total of 3 times.

RIBBING PATTERN

Alternate k1, p1.

DECREASES

Centered double decrease (cdd): Slip 2 sts together knitwise, knit the next stitch, and pass the two slipped sts over.

Instructions

With the longest circular needle and A, CO 440 sts, join into round, and work 2 rnds in Garter st. After this, place a marker directly onto the 110th, 220th, 330th, and 440th sts (4 center sts).

Work the following rnds as: *109 sts in Stockinette in Colorwork patt from chart on page 102, slip 1 st purlwise, repeat from * to end of rnd 3 times more.

From the next rnd on, for shaping, continue as follows: *Work in Stockinette st in Colorwork patt from chart to 1 st before the next center (marked) st, work a cdd with working yarn in active color, repeat from * to end of rnd 3 times more—8 decreases in each round. After all decreases, make sure that the following sts end up atop the corresponding sts of the previous rnd according to charted colorwork pattern. If you have not enough sts to comfortably fit the cord, change to shorter circular. Repeat these decreases alternatingly in every 2nd and 4th rnd, 42 times more. After 134 rnds of Stockinette in Colorwork patt, 96 sts remain on the needles.

SIZE

One size = S–L
Circumference at bust level: 53 in (135 cm)

MATERIALS

#4 medium-weight yarn in 5 colors; shown in Schachenmayr Wool 85; 100% superwash wool; 93 yd (85 m), 1.75 oz (50 g) per skein; A: #202 Nature, 14.1 oz (400 g), B: #211 Beaver Heathered, 7 oz (200 g), C: #204 Sisal Heathered, 5.3 oz (150 g), D: #225 Orange, 1.75 oz (50 g), and E: #232 Burgundy, 1.75 oz (50 g)

US 8 (5.0 mm) circular needles, in lengths 32 in (80 cm), 48 in (120 cm), and 98 in (250 cm)

4 removable stitch markers

GAUGE

Stockinette st on US 8 (5.0 mm) needles, 20 sts and 21 rows = 4 in x 4 in (10 cm x 10 cm)

COLORWORK CHART

Page 102

● ● ●

For the collar, with short circular needle and A, work another 4¾ in (12 cm) (= 28 rnds) in Ribbing patt, then BO all sts.

FINISHING

Soak the poncho in lukewarm water and carefully press out excess water. Spread out on a soft surface, block to measurements, and let dry. Hide all ends.

Prepare fringe, made of 4 strands in A, each 10 in (25 cm) in length, and attach 4 sts apart along edge of poncho.

GRETA

Pretty patterned bands

STOCKINETTE STITCH
In rounds: Knit all sts in all rounds.

RIBBING PATTERN
Rnd 1: *P1, k3, rep from * to end of rnd.
Rnd 2: P2, *k1, p3, rep from * to last 2 sts, k1, p1.
Repeat Rnds 1–2.

SIZES
S/M and L/XL
Numbers for size S/M are listed before the slash, for size L/XL after the slash. If only one number is given, it applies to both sizes.
Circumference at bust: 48½ in (123 cm)/55 in (140 cm)
Length: 23 in (58 cm)/24 in (61 cm)

MATERIALS
#4 medium-weight yarn in 6 colors; shown in Schoppel In Silk; 75% wool, 25% silk; 219 yd (200 m), 3.5 oz (100 g) per skein; A: #3681 Plum, 14.1 oz (400 g)/21.2 oz (600 g), B: #3543 Lilac, 3.5 oz (100 g), C: #5990 Petrol, 3.5 oz (100 g), D: #4193 Navy, 3.5 oz (100 g), E: #2593 Burgundy, 3.5 oz (100 g), and F: #9220 Light Grey Heathered, 3.5 oz (100 g)

US 8 (5.0 mm) circular needles, in lengths 24 in (60 cm), 40 in (100 cm), and 48 in (120 cm)

US 8 (5.0 mm) set of DPNs

GAUGE
Stockinette st on US 8 (5.0 mm) needles, 17 sts and 24 rows = 4 in x 4 in (10 cm x 10 cm)

COLORWORK CHART
Page 102

FAIR-ISLE PATTERN

Work all rnds in Stockinette according to Colorwork Chart. When changing colors, cross strands on the back of the work to avoid holes. Work the pattern repeat (10 sts wide) all the time, working Rows 1–18 once.

Instructions

Using DPNs and A, CO 104/128 sts, evenly distribute sts onto DPNs, and join into round.

Work 32/36 rnds in Ribbing patt.

After this, work 1 rnd as follows: *P11/14, p2tog, rep from * to end of rnd—96/120 sts.

Continue in Stockinette st in rnds. As number of sts on needles increases, change to longer circular needle when needed.

After 6/8 rnds of Stockinette, work first increase rnd as follows: *K6/4, M1R, rep from * to end of rnd—112/150 sts.

Work another 6 rnds in Stockinette, then work second increase rnd as follows: *K2/3, M1R, rep from * to end of rnd—168/200 sts.

Work another 8/10 rnds in Stockinette, then work third increase rnd: *K4/5, M1R, rep from * to end of rnd—210/240 sts.

Work 6 more rnds in Stockinette in A, then 18 rnds in Stockinette with Fair-Isle patt according to Colorwork Chart.

Continue in A, working 6 rnds in Stockinette, then work fourth increase rnd as follows: *K7/8, M1R, rep from * to end of rnd— 240/270 sts.

Work 18 more rnds in Stockinette, then work fifth increase rnd as follows: *K12/27, M1R, rep from * to end of rnd—260/280 sts.

Work another 40/42 rnds in Stockinette in A, then repeat 18 rnds in Stockinette with charted Fair-Isle Colorwork patt once.

In A, work 6 more rnds in Stockinette.

Purl 1 rnd as folding line, then work 6 more rnds in Stockinette. Bind off all sts loosely.

FINISHING

Fold bottom edge inwards along fold row and sew on with invisible sts. Hide all ends.

Soak the poncho in lukewarm water and carefully press out excess water. Spread out on a soft surface, block to measurements, and let dry. Hide all ends.

SIZE

One size = S–XXL
Neck circumference: 16½ in (42 cm)
Width: 48 in (120 cm)

MATERIALS

#3 light-weight yarn; shown in Lang Yarns
Cashmere Premium; 100% cashmere; 126 yd (115
m), 0.9 oz (25 g) per skein; A: #04 Black, 14.1 oz
(400 g)

#4 medium-weight metallic yarn; shown in Lang
Yarns Lamé; polyester/rayon blend; 93 yd (85 m),
0.9 oz (25 g) per skein; B: #221 Silver, 0.9 oz (25 g)

US 4 (3.5 mm) circular knitting needles, in lengths
16 in (40 cm) and 48 in (120 cm)

2 spare needles

4 transparent glass buttons, approx. ½ in (12 mm)

GAUGE

With A in Stockinette st on US 4 (3.5 mm) needles,
21 sts and 32 rows = 4 in x 4 in (10 cm x 10 cm)

ASHLEY

Refined with sparkling highlights

STOCKINETTE STITCH
Knit on RS, purl on WS.

GARTER STITCH
Knit on RS and on WS.

SQUARE PATTERN
In RS and WS rows: Alternate 3 sts in A, 3 sts in B, ending with 3 sts in A.

PATTERN SEQUENCE
4 rows Garter st in A, 2 rows Stockinette st in B, 2 rows Stockinette st in A, 4 rows Stockinette st in Square patt, 2 rows Stockinette st in A, 2 rows Stockinette st in B, 4 rows Garter st in A (20 rows total).

Instructions

FRONT
With long circular needle and A, CO 253 sts and work 20 rows in the following sequence: 5 sts Garter st in A, 243 sts in Patt Sequence, 5 sts Garter st in A. At the left Garter edge of rows worked exclusively in B, work from a second black skein. After completing the 20 Patt Sequence rows, continue in A over the middle 243 sts in Stockinette, keeping 5 sts each at the right and left edge of the piece in Garter st. After 18½ in (47 cm) (= 150 rows) total length, BO 6 sts each at both sides for shoulder sloping once, then, in every other row, BO 7 sts each at both sides 14 times more—45 sts. At 21¾ in (55 cm) (= 178 rows) total length, transfer all sts to a spare needle for holding.

BACK
Work the same as the Front, but with added slit in the back. For this, after 20 in (51 cm) (= 164 rows) total length, BO the middle 3 sts and continue both sides separately. Bind off for shoulder sloping as on Front, and after 21¾ in (55 cm) (= 178 rows) total length, transfer the 21 remaining sts for each shoulder to a spare needle for holding.

FINISHING
Graft shoulder seams in Kitchener stitch.

Starting to the left of the back slit, take up the formerly held sts of Back and Front with a short circular, and work 1 WS row in purl over all sts. Work an additional 20 rows in Patt Sequence, then BO all sts.

For the button band, pick up and knit 27 sts along the long side of the right back slit and work 5 rows Garter st. BO all sts.

For the buttonhole band, pick up and knit 27 sts accordingly along the long side of the left back slit and knit 2 rows. In Row 3, make four buttonholes as follows: k3, *yo, k2tog, k4, repeat from * 3 times more. Work 2 rows more in Garter st, then BO all sts. Place buttonhole band atop button band, and sew narrow sides with invisible stitching to the 3 bound-off sts of the Back. Sew buttons onto button band according to buttonhole placement. Hide all ends.

VIVIEN

A pretty lace edging enhances stripes

STOCKINETTE STITCH

In rows: Knit on RS, purl on WS.
In rounds: Knit all sts in all rounds.

GARTER STITCH

In rows: Knit on RS and on WS.
In rounds: Alternate 1 knit round, 1 purl round.

EDGING PATTERN

Row 1 (RS) and all other RS rows: Knit.
Row 2: K3, k2tog, yo, k2tog, yo, k1, yo, k2—11 sts.
Row 4: K2, *k2tog, yo, repeat from * once, k3, yo, k2—12 sts.

Row 6: K1, *k2tog, yo, repeat from * once, k5, yo, k2—13 sts.
Row 8: K3, *yo, k2tog, repeat from * once, k1, k2tog, yo, k2tog, k1—12 sts.
Row 10: K4, yo, k2tog, yo, k3tog, yo, k2tog, k1—11 sts.
Row 12: K5, yo, k3tog, yo, k2tog, k1—10 sts.
Repeat Rows 1–12.

STRIPE SEQUENCE

*14 rnds B, 6 rnds A, rep from * 2 times more, 14 rnds B, 14 rnds A, **6 rnds B, 14 rnds A, rep from ** 2 times more (148 rnds total).

Instructions

For the collar, in A and with short circular needle, CO 116 sts, join into round, and work 20 rnds in Garter st. After this, work 1 rnd in B as follows: k1, place marker, *k28, pm, k1, pm, rep from * 2 times more, k28, pm.

Continue in Stockinette in Stripe Sequence, starting increases immediately in Rnd 1 as follows: k1, sm, M1R, *knit to next marker, M1L, sm, k1, sm, M1R, rep from * 2 times more, knit to last marker, M1L, sm.

Repeat increases in every other rnd, 10 times more, then in every 6th rnd, 21 times more (always 8 increases per increase rnd). After 21 in (53 cm) (= 148 rnds) from beginning of Stripe Sequence, there are 372 sts on the needles. Work 1 rnd more, removing all markers. Do not bind off, but leave live sts on the needle.

SIZE

One size = SM–XL
Circumference at bust: 57 in
(145 cm)

MATERIALS

#4 medium-weight yarn in 2 colors; shown in Lang Yarns Yak; 50% yak, 50% merino wool; 142 yd (130 m), 1.75 oz (50 g) per skein; A: #39 Bark, 10.6 oz (300 g), and B: #48 Rosewood, 7 oz (200 g)

US 7 (4.5 mm) circular knitting needles, in lengths 24 in (60 cm), 48 in (120 cm), and 79 in (200 cm)

US 6 (4.0 mm) set of DPNs

8 ring stitch markers

US G/6 (4.0 mm) crochet hook

Piece of contrasting color yarn for provisional cast-on

Spare needle

GAUGE

Stockinette stitch on US 7 (4.5 mm) needles, 18 sts and 28 rows = 4 in x 4 in (10 cm x 10 cm)

For the Edging, using crochet hook and contrasting color scrap yarn, crochet a chain of 14. Break working yarn and pull it through the last st. With a DPN and in A, pick up and knit 10 sts from the crocheted chain, take up a second DPN, and work in Edging Pattern in back-and-forth rows with turning, at the same time always knitting together the last Edging st with the first st of the poncho in every RS row. After 743 rows, 1 poncho st remains. Knit this last remaining st together with the last 2 Edging sts (you will work a k3tog). After 744 rows (Rows 1–12 of the Edging patt will have been worked 62 times total), all sts of the body of the poncho will have been used up. Now, carefully pull out the crocheted chain while taking up the freed sts with a spare needle. Graft the live Edging sts in Kitchener stitch.

FINISHING
Soak the poncho in lukewarm water and carefully press out excess water. Spread out on a soft surface, block to measurements, and let dry. Hide all ends.

FINJA
Beautifully cabled

STOCKINETTE STITCH
In rounds: Knit all sts in all rounds.

RIBBING PATTERN
Alternate k2, p2.

CABLE PATTERN
Work from chart on page 105. Shown are only odd-numbered rnds; in even-numbered rnds, work all sts as they appear (knit the knits and purl the purls), knit the slipped sts. Work the patt rep (24 sts wide) once per rnd, repeating Rows 1–12 height-wise.

Instructions

The poncho is worked from the top down in the round.

With DPN set, CO 80 sts and evenly distribute sts onto DPNs. Join into round and work 10 rnds in Ribbing patt. Knit 2 rnds, at the same time in Rnd 2 increasing 16 sts as follows: *k5, M1L, rep from * to end of rnd—96 sts.

SIZE
One size = S–L
Circumference at bust: 57 in (145 cm)
Length: 19 in (48 cm)

MATERIALS
#4 medium-weight yarn; shown in Schoppel Albmerino; 100% wool; 110 yd (100 m), 1.75 oz (50 g) per skein; #9263 Grey Heathered, 15.9 oz (450 g)

US 8 (5.0 mm) circular needles, in lengths 24 in (60 cm), 40 in (100 cm), and 48 in (120 cm)

US 8 (5.0 mm) set of DPNs

Cable needle

8 ring stitch markers

GAUGE
Stockinette st on US 8 (5.0 mm) needles, 16 sts and 18 rows = 4 in x 4 in (10 cm x 10 cm)

CHART
Page 105

● ● ●

Change to short circular needle, and in the next rnd, divide sts as follows, placing markers on the needle where indicated: k1, pm, k22, pm, k2, pm, k11, pm, work 24 sts in Cable patt from chart, pm, k11, pm, k2, pm, k22, pm, k1.

Continue as follows:

Rnd 1: K1, sm, M1L, knit to next marker, M1R, sm, k2, sm, M1L, knit to next marker, M1R, sm, work 24 sts in Cable patt, sm, M1L, knit to next marker, M1R, sm, k2, sm, M1L, knit to next marker, M1R, sm, k1.

Rnd 2: Knit to beginning of cable section while slipping all markers, work 24 sts in Cable patt, knit to end of rnd, slipping all markers.

Work Rnds 1 and 2 24 times more—296 sts. There will be 8 increases each in every other rnd.

Continue as follows:

Rnd 3: K1, sm, knit to next marker, M1R, sm, k2, sm, M1L, k to next m, sm, work 24 sts in Cable patt, sm, knit to next marker, M1R, sm, k2, sm, M1L, knit to next marker, sm, k1.

Rnd 4: Same as Rnd 2.

Repeat Rnds 3 and 4 33 times more—432 sts. There will be 4 increases each in every other rnd.

After this, work another 12 rnds without increases in the following manner, removing all markers: work in Ribbing patt to beginning of Cable patt, work 24 sts in Cable patt, work Ribbing patt to end of rnd.

BO all sts.

FINISHING

Soak the poncho in lukewarm water and carefully press out excess water. Spread out on a soft surface, block to measurements, and let dry. Hide all ends.

RABEA

Classy in black and white

RIBBING PATTERN 1
In RS rows: Alternate k1, p1.
In WS rows: Work all sts as they appear (knit the knits and purl the purls).

RIBBING PATTERN 2
In RS rows: Alternate p1, k1.
In WS rows: Work all sts as they appear (knit the knits and purl the purls).

STOCKINETTE STITCH
Knit on RS, purl on WS.

DIAMOND PATTERN
Work from Charts A and B. To better demonstrate the stitch pattern, charts show RS and WS rows as viewed from the right side of the knitted fabric. Accordingly, sts shown as "knit" are purled in WS rows and sts shown as "purl" are knitted in WS rows (please also refer to knitting symbol legend). Start with the st(s) shown before the patt rep, repeat the pattern rep (8 sts wide) as long as you have enough sts, and end with the st(s) shown after the pattern rep. Repeat Rows 1–10.

Instructions

FRONT
In B, CO 47 sts, then, in A, CO 224 sts more—271 sts. In this color sequence, work 6 rows in Ribbing patt 1.

From the next row on, work in the following sequence:

In A, work 6 sts in Ribbing patt 1 and 218 sts in Diamond patt from Chart A, then in B, work 41 sts in Stockinette and 6 sts in Ribbing patt 2—271 sts. Continue in this manner. Where color B meets color A, gradually decrease the number of A sts as shown in the chart, and increase the number of B sts accordingly (B sts will be continually shifted by 1 st to the right in every other row once, and by 1 st in every Row 1 three times).

SIZE
One size = S–XXL
Measurements: 45¾ in x 20 in (116 cm x 50 cm)

MATERIALS
#3 light-weight yarn in 2 colors; shown in Schachenmayr Merino Extrafine; 100% merino wool; 131 yd (120 m), 1.75 oz (50 g) per skein; A: #101 White, 17.6 oz (500 g), and B: #199 Black, 12.3 oz (350 g)

US 6 (4.0 mm) circular needle, 48 in (120 cm) long
US G/6 (4.0 mm) crochet hook

GAUGE
Diamond patt from Chart A or B with US 6 (4.0 mm) needles, 23 sts and 30 rows = 4 in x 4 in (10 cm x 10 cm)

CHARTS
Page 105

● ● ●

After 13½ in (34.5 cm) (= 104 rows) in Diamond patt, for shoulder sloping, BO 6 sts each at both sides once, then, in every other row, on both sides, BO 5 sts each, 19 times total.

At the same time, at height 14½ in (36.5 cm) (= 110 rows) from beginning of Diamond patt (there are 121 sts in color A and 118 sts in color B on the needle), BO the center stitch for the neckline and continue both sides separately. For V-neck shaping, BO 2 sts each on both sides in every other row 8 times more, then in every other row, alternatingly BO 1 st once and 2 sts once, 4 times in all. After 19 in (48 cm) (= 144 rows) from beginning of Diamond patt, BO rem 6 sts.

BACK

Work the same as the front, but mirror-inverted: In A, CO 224, then in B, CO 47. In this color sequence, work 6 rows in Ribbing patt 1.

From the next row on, work in the following sequence: In B, work 6 sts in Ribbing patt 1 and 41 sts in Stockinette, then in A, 218 sts according to Chart B, and 6 sts in Ribbing patt 2.

Continue in this manner, working shoulder shaping and V-neck decreases the same as for the front.

FINISHING

Close shoulder seams. Work crocheted edging around the neckline, matching up colors A and B as appropriate: 1 rnd of sc and 1 rnd crab stitch (i.e., sc worked from left to right).

NORA

Intricate cables

RIBBING PATTERN

In RS rows: Alternate k1, p1.
In WS rows: Work all sts as they appear (knit the knits and purl the purls).
In rounds: Alternate k1, p1.

REVERSE STOCKINETTE

RS rows: Purl all sts.
WS rows: Knit all sts.

CABLE PATTERN

Work from Chart A. Only RS rows are shown; in WS rows, work all sts as they appear, purl all slipped sts.

Work the pattern repeat (32 sts wide) 2 times. Repeat Rows 1–22 a total of 12 times, then work only Rows 1 and 2 once more.

BIAS STRIPE PATTERN

Work from Chart B. Only RS rows are shown; in WS rows, work all sts as they appear (knit the knits and purl the purls). Work the pattern repeat (8 sts wide) all the time, ending with the sts after the pattern repeat. Repeat Rows 1–16 a total of 16 times, then work only Rows 1–10 once more.

SIZE

One size
Rectangles: 21¾ in x 45 in (55 cm x 114 cm)

MATERIALS

#4 medium-weight yarn; shown in Schachenmayr Wool 85; 100% superwash wool; 93 yd (85 m), 1.75 oz (50 g) per skein; #294 Fog, 24.8 oz (700 g)

US 8 (5.0 mm) circular needles, in lengths 24 in (60 cm) and 32 in (80 cm)

Cable needle

2 removable stitch markers

GAUGE

Bias Stripe patt with US 8 (5.0 mm) needles,
18 sts and 24 rows = 4 in x 4 in (10 cm x 10 cm)

Cable patt with US 8 (5.0 mm) needles,
32 sts and 22 rows (1 pattern repeat) = 6 in (15.5 cm)

CHARTS

Page 105

● ● ○

Instructions

For first half of poncho, using long circular needle, CO 106 sts and, for the edging, work 8 rows in Ribbing patt, then continue as follows: 2 sts reverse Stockinette, 64 sts in Cable patt from Chart A, 36 sts in Bias Stripe patt from Chart B, 4 sts in Ribbing patt. Continue to work even in this pattern. After 45 in (114 cm) (= 274 rows) total length, BO all sts.

Work the second half of the poncho the same way.

FINISHING

Soak the two rectangles in lukewarm water, carefully press out excess water, and spread out both pieces on a soft surface to block and let dry.

After this, sew both pieces together as follows: Place the first half of the poncho right side up on the floor so that the ribbing on the narrow side is located at the bottom. Now, put the second half, also right side up, on the floor sideways, so that the narrow side without ribbing meets the bottom part of the first piece (see schematic), and sew both pieces together. Now, rotate the top narrow edge of the first piece clockwise until it completely borders the bottom part of the second piece, then sew it on.

With the short circular needle, pick up and knit sts from the neckline edge as follows: 1 st from the first corner of the V-neck, 99 sts to the next corner, 1 st from the second corner of the V-neck, 99 sts to the first corner—200 sts. Mark both corner sts using removable markers. Work in the round as follows:

Rnd 1: All sts in Ribbing patt—200 sts.

Rnd 2: K1, k2tog, cont in Ribbing patt to 2 sts before the next marker, sk2p, k1, k2tog, cont in Ribbing patt to last 2 sts of rnd, sk2p—196 sts.

Rnd 3: Knit the knits and purl the purls.

Rnd 4: K1, p2tog-tbl, cont in Ribbing patt to 2 sts before the next marker, p2tog, k1, p2tog-tbl, cont in Ribbing patt to last 2 sts of rnd, p2tog—192 sts.

Rnd 5: Knit the knits and purl the purls.

Repeat Rnds 2–5 once more—184 sts. Then BO all sts. Hide all ends.

sew together

sew together

SIZE

One size = S–XXL
Measurements: 51¼ in x 18 in (130 cm x 46 cm)

MATERIALS

#3 light-weight yarn in 2 colors; shown in Lang Yarns Merino 120; 100% wool; 131 yd (120 m), 1.75 oz (50 g) per skein; A: #04 Black, 19.4 oz (550 g), and B: #198 Kiwi, 19.4 oz (550 g)

US 10¾ (7.0 mm) circular needle, 40 in (100 cm) long

2 spare needles

Crochet hook for attaching fringe

GAUGE

Stockinette st on US 10 ¾ (7.0 mm) needles with yarn held double, 14 sts and 20 rows = 4 in x 4 in (10 cm x 10 cm)

FRIA

Evenly striped

STOCKINETTE STITCH
Knit all sts on RS, purl all sts on WS.

GARTER STITCH
Knit all sts on RS and WS.

PATTERN SEQUENCE 1
Rows 1–6: With A held double, work 12 sts in Garter st, 104 sts in Stockinette, 12 sts Garter st.
Rows 7–8: With B held double, work 128 sts in Garter st.
Repeat Rows 1–8.

PATTERN SEQUENCE 2
Rows 1–2: With A held double, work 128 sts Garter st.
Rows 3–8: With B held double, work 12 sts Garter st, 104 sts Stockinette, 12 sts Garter st.

Instructions

The poncho is worked sideways in one piece as follows: With A held double, CO 128 sts and work 4 rows in Garter st, then cont in Patt Sequence 1. After 20 in (50 cm) (= 100 rows) in Patt Sequence 1, divide work for the neckline and continue both sides separately. For this, transfer the last 64 sts to a spare needle for holding, and work over the first 64 sts only.

Holding 1 strand A and B together, continue as follows: 12 sts Garter st, 52 sts in Stockinette, then for the collar, CO an additional 16 sts (80 sts total). Continue in this pattern, working the 16 collar sts in Garter st. After 11 in (28 cm) (= 55 rows) from separation, in a WS row, BO the 16 collar sts and transfer the remaining 64 sts to a spare needle for holding.

Now, take up the formerly held last 64 sts on the other side again with the circular, and continue holding 1 strand each of color A and B together: CO an additional 16 sts for the collar, then work 52 sts in Stockinette, 12 sts in Garter. Continue in this pattern, working the 16 collar sts in Garter st. After 11 in (28 cm) (= 56 rows) from separation, in a RS row, BO the 16 collar sts.

Take up the formerly held 64 sts at the other side with the circular needle, and continue over all 128 sts in Patt Sequence 2. After 20 in (50 cm) (= 100 rows) in Patt Sequence 2, with B held double, work another 4 rows Garter st, then BO all sts.

FINISHING
Join the sides of the collar with mattress stitch.

Soak the poncho in lukewarm water and carefully press out excess water. Spread out on a soft surface, block to measurements, and let dry. Hide all ends.

At the right and left edge (cast-on and bind-off row), attach fringe with a crochet hook, 6 strands of 12 in (30 cm) length each, approx. 1½ in (4 cm) apart, as follows: At the CO edge of color A, use color B fringe, and at the BO edge of color B, use color A fringe.

SIZE

One size = S–L
Circumference at bust: 55 in (140 cm)

MATERIALS

#3 light-weight yarn; shown in Rowan
Truesilk; 100% silk; 164 yd (150 m), 1.75
oz (50 g) per skein; #339 Sleep, 14.1 oz
(400 g)

US 6 (4.0 mm) circular needles, in lengths
32 in (80 cm), 40 in (100 cm), and 48 in
(120 cm)

Cable needle

Spare needle

Piece of waste yarn in contrasting color for
provisional cast-on

US G/6 (4.0 mm) crochet hook

GAUGE

Stockinette st on US 6 (4.0 mm) needles,
23 sts and 32 rows = 4 in x 4 in (10 cm x
10 cm)

CHART

Page 104

MILA

Delicate and romantic

STOCKINETTE STITCH
In rounds: Knit all sts in all rounds.

GARTER STITCH
In rounds: Alternate knit 1 rnd, purl 1 rnd.

PATTERN SEQUENCE
Alternate 6 rnds Garter Stitch with 5 rnds Stockinette.

CABLE PATTERN
Work from chart on page 104. Only RS rows are shown; in WS rows, except for the selv sts, work all sts as they appear (knit the knits and purl the purls). Begin with the sts before the pattern repeat, work the pattern rep (16 sts wide, with gray background) 3 times, and end with the sts after the pattern rep. Work Rows 1–36 of the chart 10 times.

SELVEDGE STITCHES
Knit the selv sts on RS and WS.

Instructions

Using crochet hook and contrasting color waste yarn, crochet a chain of 80. With short circular needle and main color yarn, pick up and knit 74 sts from this crocheted chain, then purl 1 WS row. Continue in Cable patt from chart. After 360 rows in Cable patt, leaving all live sts on the needles, carefully pull out the provisional crocheted chain, placing the freed sts on a spare needle. Right side facing out, join the cabled strip into a round so that live sts are placed opposite each other. Now, graft sts in Kitchener stitch.

Place the cabled strip sideways so that the beginning sts (sts before the pattern repeat) are now at the top. From the selv sts, pick up and knit 320 sts, evenly spaced, and continue in the round in indicated Patt Sequence.

After 9 rnds, work first decrease rnd as follows: *k6, k2tog, repeat from * 39 times more—280 sts.

Work another 18 rnds in Patt Sequence, then work next decrease rnd: *k5, k2tog, repeat from * 39 times more—240 sts.

Work another 13 rnds in Patt Sequence, then work next decrease rnd: *k4, k2tog, repeat from * 39 times more—200 sts.

Work another 7 rnds in Patt Sequence, then work next decrease rnd: *k3, k2tog, repeat from * 39 times more—160 sts.

Work another 3 rnds in Patt Sequence, then work next decrease rnd: *k2, k2tog, repeat from * 39 times more—120 sts.

Work another 6 rnds in Patt Sequence, then BO all sts.

FINISHING
Soak the poncho in lukewarm water, carefully press out excess water, and place on a soft surface for blocking. Hide all ends.

ALIDA

Magical gradient

STOCKINETTE STITCH

Knit on RS, purl on WS.

RIBBING PATTERN

RS rows: Alternate k1, p1.
WS rows: Knit the knits and purl the purls.

Instructions

CO 194 sts and work 8 rows in Ribbing patt. Continue in the following pattern sequence: 6 sts Ribbing patt, 182 sts Stockinette, 6 sts Ribbing patt (starting with p1).

After 23¼ in (59 cm) (= 140 rows) total length, continue both sides separately, starting with the right half: 6 sts Ribbing patt, 91 sts Stockinette, transfer remaining 97 sts of the left half to a spare needle for holding. Turn work to WS, k1, p2tog, work in Patt Sequence to end of row. Work another RS row in Patt Sequence, then work the next WS row again the same way as the previous one—95 sts. Place all sts on a spare needle for holding.

With circular needle, take up the formerly held 97 sts of the left half and work Row 1 (RS) as: k1, sk2p. Work 1 WS row in Patt Sequence, then work next RS row again the same way as the previous one—95 sts. After this, continue over all sts in Stockinette, keeping the last 6 sts in Ribbing patt as before. At 29 in (74 cm) (= 185 rows) from separation (ending having just worked a RS row), rotate work so that all sts are located exactly above the held sts of the right half, with the RS of the fabric facing up, and both needle tips pointing to the right. Graft the 95 sts of the left half together with the 95 sts of the right half in Kitchener stitch.

FINISHING

Soak the poncho in lukewarm water and carefully press out excess water. Spread out on a soft surface, block to measurements, and let dry. Hide all ends.

SIZE

One size = S–L
Back length: Approx. 24 in (60 cm)
Front length: Approx. 20 in (50 cm)

MATERIALS

#3 light-weight gradient yarn with long color repeats; shown in Schoppel Gradient; 100% merino wool; 284 yd (260 m), 3.5 oz (100 g) per skein; #2262 Fan Curve, 17.6 oz (500 g)

US 6 (4.0 mm) circular needle, 32 in (80 cm) long

2 spare needles

Tapestry needle

GAUGE

Stockinette st on US 6 (4.0 mm) needles,
19 sts and 25 rows = 4 in x 4 in (10 cm x 10 cm)

STELLA

Light and airy

SIZE

One size = S–XXL
Measurements: 39½ in x 25½
in (100 cm x 65 cm)

MATERIALS

#3 light-weight yarn; shown in
Schoppel Cashmere Queen;
45% wool, 35% cashmere, 20%
silk; 153 yd (140 m), 1.75 oz
(50 g) per skein; #2965 Plum,
15.9 oz (450 g)

US 6 (4.0 mm) circular needle,
32 in (80 cm) long

GAUGE

Openwork Pattern with US 6
(4.0 mm) needles, 15 sts and
26 rows = 4 in x 4 in (10 cm x
10 cm)

● ● ○

CABLE PATTERN

Row 1: P2, *slip 1 st knitwise, k2, then pass the
slipped st over both sts, p2, rep from * to end
of row.

Row 2: K2, *p1, yo, p1, k2, rep from * to end of
row.

Row 3: P2, *k3, p2, rep from * to end of row.

Row 4: K2, *p3, k2, rep from * to end of row.
Repeat Rows 1–4.

OPENWORK PATTERN

Row 1: Purl.

Row 2: Knit.

Row 3: K2, *slip 1 st purlwise with yarn in back,
k1, rep from * to end of row.

Row 4: *K1, slip 1 st purlwise with yarn in front,
rep from * to last 2 sts, k2.

Row 5: K1, *yo, k2tog, rep from * to last st, k1.

Row 6: Purl.
Repeat Rows 1–6.

Instructions

CO 97 sts and work 10 rows in Cable patt (the
last row will be Row 2 of the pattern).

After this, continue in the following manner: 84
sts in Openwork patt, slip 1 st, 12 sts in Cable
patt.

After 506 rows Openwork patt (Rows 1–6 of the
Openwork patt will have been worked 84
times, and Rows 1–2 once), work 10 rows in
Cable patt over all sts. Bind off all sts loosely.

FINISHING

Soak the piece in lukewarm water and carefully
press out excess water. Spread out on a soft
surface, block to measurements, and let dry.
Fold the rectangle in half widthwise, RS facing
out. Sew the edges without Cable patt edging
with mattress stitch, starting at the bottom
edge and keeping the upper 14½ in (37 cm)
open for the neckline. Hide all ends.

ROMY

Poncho with matching cowl

GARTER STITCH
In rounds: Alternate knit 1 rnd, purl 1 rnd.

SLIP STITCH PATTERN
Rnd 1: With A, knit all sts.
Rnd 2: With A, purl all sts.
Rnds 3–4: With B, *slip 2 sts purlwise, k2, rep from * to end of rnd.
Rnds 5–8: Repeat Rnds 1–4 once.
Rnd 9: With B, knit all sts.
Rnd 10: With B, purl all sts.
Rnds 11–12: With A, *slip 2 sts purlwise, k2, rep from * to end of rnd.
Rnds 13–16: Repeat Rnds 9–12 once.
Repeat Rnds 1–16.

SIZE
One size = S–L
Circumference at bust: 51¼ in (130 cm)
Cowl: 59 in (150 cm) circumference x 8 in (20 cm) high

MATERIALS
#2 fine-weight yarn in 2 colors; shown in Schoppel Life Style; 169½ yd (155 m), 1.75 oz (50 g) per skein; A: #6345 Khaki, 19.4 oz (550 g), and B: #1862 Wild Roses, 5.3 oz (150 g)

US 4 (3.5 mm) circular knitting needles, in lengths 24 in (60 cm), 32 in (80 cm), and 48 in (120 cm)
US 4 (3.5 mm) set of DPNs

GAUGE
Garter st with US 4 (3.5 mm) needles, 24 sts and 45 rows = 4 in x 4 in (10 cm x 10 cm)

Slip Stitch patt with US 4 (3.5 mm needles, 26 sts and 52 rows = 4 in x 4 in (10 cm x 10 cm)

● ● ○

Instructions

PONCHO
Using the longest circular needle and A, CO 292 sts and join into round. Work 16 rnds in Slip Stitch patt, then continue in A in Garter st, decreasing 2 sts evenly spaced in Rnd 1—290 sts.

After 10¾ in (27.5 cm) (= 124 rows) Garter st, work first decrease rnd as follows: *k27, k2tog, repeat from * 9 times more—280 sts.

Work 9 rnds in Garter st, then continue as follows (changing to next shorter circular or DPNs as stitch count decreases):

Decrease Rnd 2: *K5, k2tog, repeat from * 39 times more—240 sts.

Work 13 rnds in Garter st.

Decrease Rnd 3: *K4, k2tog, repeat from * 39 times more—200 sts.

Work 13 rnds in Garter st.

Decrease Rnd 4: *K3, k2tog, repeat from * 39 times more—160 sts.

Work 11 rnds in Garter st.

Decrease Rnd 5: *K6, k2tog, repeat from * 19 times more—140 sts.

Work 9 rnds in Garter st.

Decrease Rnd 6: *K5, k2tog, repeat from * 19 times more—120 sts.

Work another 7 rnds in Garter st, then BO all sts.

COWL
Using long circular needle and A, CO 388 sts and join into round. Work 104 rnds in Slip Stitch patt, then BO all sts.

FINISHING
Soak both pieces in lukewarm water and carefully press out excess water. Spread out on a soft surface, block to measurements, and let dry. Hide all ends.

JARA

Naturally beautiful

SIZES

S–L and XL–XXL

Numbers for size S–L are listed before the slash, for size XL–XXL after the slash. If only one number is given, it applies to both sizes.

Circumference at bust: 49¼ in (125 cm)/57 in (145 cm)

Length: 22 in (56 cm)/23½ in (60 cm)

MATERIALS

#5 bulky-weight yarn; shown in Schoppel Pur; 100% merino wool; 164 yd (150 m), 3.5 oz (100 g) per skein; #1659

Oxyde, 14.1 oz (400 g)/21.2 oz (600 g)

US 10 (6.0 mm) circular needle, 32 in (80 cm) long

GAUGE

In Double Seed st on US 10 (6.0 mm) needles, 13 sts and 20 rows = 4 in x 4 in (10 cm x 10 cm)

● ○ ○

DOUBLE SEED STITCH

Row 1: *K1, p1, repeat from * to last st, k1.
Row 2: Knit the knits and purl the purls.
Row 3: *P1, k1, repeat from * to last st, p1.
Row 4: Knit the knits and purl the purls.
Repeat Rows 1–4.

Instructions

CO 73/79 sts and work for 49¼ in (125 cm)/57 in (145 cm) (= 248/292 rows) in Double Seed st. BO all sts.

FINISHING

Soak the poncho in lukewarm water and carefully press out excess water. Spread out on a soft surface, block to measurements, and let dry. Hide all ends.

Fold poncho in half lengthwise so that long sides are atop each other. At one side, starting at the cast-on edge, sew edges together in mattress stitch over a length of 12¼ in (31 cm)/14½ in (37 cm), leaving a neck opening of 12½ in (31.5 cm)/14 in (35.5 cm). Leave the other side open. Hide all ends.

FIONA
With ruffled edge

STOCKINETTE STITCH
In rounds: Knit all sts in all rounds.

BOBBLE
Work [p1, k1, p1, k1] into the same stitch. Now, one after another, pass the second, third and fourth st over the first st and off the needle.

RIBBING PATTERN
Rnd 1: K2, *p2, bobble, p2, k3, rep from * to last 6 sts, p2, bobble, p2, k1.
Rnd 2: Knit the knits and purl the purls; knit the bobbles.
Rnd 3: K2, *p5, k3, rep from * to last 6 sts, p5, k1.
Rnd 4: Work the same as Rnd 2.
Repeat Rnds 1–4 once, then work only Rnd 1 once (9 rnds total).

BELL PATTERN
Work from chart. Only odd-numbered rounds are shown; in even-numbered rnds, work all sts as they appear (knit the knits and purl the purls); knit the yo's through the back loop. Work the pattern repeat (at beginning, 8 sts) around, working Rnds 1–14 once.

PATTERN SEQUENCE
*9 rnds in Ribbing patt, 20 rnds in Stockinette, repeat from * 4 times more, then work another 9 rnds in Ribbing patt (154 rnds total).

Instructions

With DPN set, CO 88 sts, evenly distribute onto DPNs, and work in indicated Patt Sequence in the round. In Rnd 10 from CO, work first increase rnd as follows: *K11, M1R, repeat from * 7 times more—96 sts.

Continue to work in Patt Sequence, working further increase rnds as follows (changing to next longer circular as stitch count increases):

Rnd 17: *K6, M1R, repeat from * 15 times more—112 sts.
Rnd 22: *K2, M1R, repeat from * 55 times more—168 sts.
Rnd 29: K2, *M1R, k5, repeat from * 3 times more, **M1R, k4, repeat from ** 30 times more, ***M1R, k5, repeat from *** 3 times more, M1R, k2—208 sts.

SIZE
One size = S–M
Circumference at bust: 49½ in (126 cm)

MATERIALS
#4 medium-weight cotton gradient ribbon yarn; shown in Lang Yarns Sol Dégradé; 100% cotton; 219 yd (200 m), 3.5 oz (100 g) per skein; #44 Limone-Aqua, 17.6 oz (500 g)

US 8 (5.0 mm) circular needles, in lengths 24 in (60 cm), 32 in (80 cm), and 48 in (120 cm)

US 8 (5.0 mm) set of DPNs

GAUGE
Stockinette st on US 8 (5.0 mm) needles, 19 sts and 28 rows = 4 in x 4 in (10 cm x 10 cm)

CHART
Page 106

Rnd 59: K3, *M1R, k7, repeat from * 7 times more, **M1R, k6, repeat from ** 14 times more, ***M1R, k7, repeat from *** 7 times more, M1R, k3—240 sts.

Continue even in this pattern without increases. After 21¾ in (55 cm) (= 154 rnds) total length, work 14 rnds more in Bell patt, then BO all sts loosely.

FINISHING

Soak the poncho in lukewarm water and carefully press out excess water. Spread out on a soft surface, block to measurements, and let dry. Hide all ends.

MELINA

Spot-on with zigzags

STOCKINETTE STITCH
In rows: Knit on RS, purl on WS.
In rounds: Knit all sts in all rounds.

RIBBING PATTERN
Alternate k1, p1.

FAIR-ISLE ZIGZAG PATTERN
Work all rnds in Stockinette according to Colorwork Chart on page 103. Repeat the pattern repeat (at beginning, 14 sts wide) across each round. In Rnds 7, 11, 17, and 21, work decreases as shown. Work Rnds 1–23 height-wise only once. When changing colors, carry floats loosely at back of work to prevent knitted fabric from constricting.

SIZE
One size = S–XL
Circumference at bust: 58 in (147 cm)

MATERIALS
#4 medium-weight linen ribbon yarn in 3 colors; shown in Lang Yarns Lino; 100% linen viscose; 120.3 yd (110 m), 1.75 oz (50 g) per skein; A: #01 White, 8.8 oz (250 g), B: #10 Blue, 1.75 oz (50 g), and C: #78 Turquoise, 3.5 oz (100 g)

US 8 (5.0 mm) circular needles, in lengths 24 in (60 cm), 32 in (80 cm), and 48 in (120 cm)

US 6 (4.0 mm) circular needle, 24 in (60 cm) long

Ring stitch marker

GAUGE
Stockinette Stitch on US 8 (5.0 mm) needles, 19 sts and 28 rows = 4 in x 4 in (10 cm x 10 cm)

COLORWORK CHART
Page 103

Instructions

Using long circular needle and A, CO 280 sts and join into round, placing a stitch marker for the beginning of the round. For ribbing, work 10 rnds in Ribbing patt, then continue in Stockinette. After 7½ in (19 cm) (= 54 rows) from ribbing, continue in Fair-Isle Zigzag patt from Colorwork Chart, starting decreases as shown in Rnd 7 of chart. As stitch count decreases, change to shorter circular.

After completion of Colorwork Chart, 200 sts remain on the needles. Knit 1 rnd in C.

Continue in Stockinette in C, first working short rows as follows:

Row 1 (RS): K130, turn work.

Row 2 (WS): Yo, p110, turn work.

Row 3: Yo, k90, turn work.

Row 4: Yo, p70, turn work.

Row 5: Yo, k50, turn work.

Row 6: Yo, p30, turn work.

After this, proceed to working over all sts again in the round as follows:

Rnd 1: Yo, k20, k2tog the yo with the next st, *k19, k2tog the yo with the next st, repeat from * once, knit to end of rnd.

Rnd 2: *K19, ssk the next st with the yo, rep from * 2 times more, knit to end of rnd.

Continue in Stockinette st in C. In the next rnd, work decrease rnd as follows: *k8, k2tog, repeat from * 19 times—180 sts.

Work 7 rnds even in Stockinette without decreases, then work next decrease rnd: *k7, k2tog, repeat from * 19 times—160 sts.

Work 7 rnds even in Stockinette without decreases, then work next decrease rnd: *k6, k2tog, repeat from * 19 times—140 sts.

Work 7 rnds even in Stockinette without decreases, then work next decrease rnd: *k5, k2tog, repeat from * 19 times—120 sts.

Work another 4 rnds even in Stockinette without decreases, then with US 6 (4.0 mm) circular needle, work another 10 rnds in Ribbing patt over all sts. BO all sts.

FINISHING

Soak the poncho in lukewarm water and carefully press out excess water. Spread out on a soft surface, block to measurements, and let dry.

CAPES

AVA
Homage to Little Red Riding Hood

STOCKINETTE STITCH
Knit on RS, purl on WS.

GARTER STITCH
Knit on RS and on WS.

LACE PATTERN
Work from Charts A and B. Only RS rows are shown; in WS rows, purl all sts and yo's.

Chart A: Start with the sts before the pattern repeat, work the pattern repeat (18 sts wide) 12 times widthwise, and end with the sts after the pattern repeat. Work Rows 1–30 once, then repeat Rows 7–30 all the time.

Chart B: Start with the sts before the pattern repeat, work the pattern repeat (at beginning, 36 sts wide) 6 times, and end with the sts after the pattern repeat. Work Rows 1–42 of chart once.

Instructions

With long circular needle, CO 235 sts and purl 1 WS row. Now, work in the following pattern sequence: 5 sts Garter st, 225 sts Lace patt from Chart A, 5 sts Garter st. After 10¾ in (27.5 cm) (= 72 rows) total length, in a RS row, work a buttonhole as follows: k2, yo, k2tog, k1, then continue in pattern sequence. In every following 12th row, work 5 more buttonholes in this manner.

At the same time, after 15¼ in (38.5 cm) (= 102 rows) total length (Rows 7–30 of Chart A have been worked 4 times), continue in the following manner: 5 sts Garter st, 225 sts Lace patt from Chart B, 5 sts Garter st. After having worked Rows 1–42 of Chart B once, 67 sts remain on the needles.

BO these sts with a crochet hook as follows: Insert crochet hook from front to back into first st, pull the working yarn through, and let the stitch slip off the left needle. Do the same with the second stitch, so that you now have 2 loops on the hook. Pull the working yarn through both loops at once (forming 1 sc). *Ch1, insert hook into next st, pull the working yarn through and remove st from left needle, then pull working yarn through both loops on the hook. Repeat from * until all sts have been bound off.

Turn work and finish the neckline by working 1 row sc and 1 row crab stitch (i.e., sc worked from left to right) while skipping the chain spaces from the crochet-BO row.

FINISHING
Soak the cape in lukewarm water and carefully press out excess water. Spread out on a soft surface, block to measurements, and let dry. Sew the buttons to the Garter Stitch button band according to the position of the buttonholes. Hide all ends.

SIZE

One size = S–L
Circumference at bust: 51¼ in
(130 cm)

MATERIALS

#2 fine-weight mohair/silk yarn;
shown in Rowan Kidsilk Haze;
70% kid mohair, 30% silk; 230 yd
(210 m), 0.9 oz (25 g) per skein;
#595 Liqueur, 2.7 oz (75 g)

US 4 (3.5 mm) circular knitting
needles, in lengths 16 in (40 cm)
and 40 in (100 cm)

6 buttons, approx. ¾ in (18 mm)

GAUGE

Stockinette st on US 5 (3.5 mm)
needles, 18 sts and 26 rows =
4 in x 4 in (10 cm x 10 cm)

CHARTS

Page 108

CELINA
Enveloped in sunny yellow

STOCKINETTE STITCH
In rounds: Knit all sts in all rounds.

HEM RIBBING
Alternate k1, p1.

RIBBING PATTERN 1
Alternate k4, p2.

RIBBING PATTERN 2
Alternate p2, k4.

CABLED RIBBING A
In all rnds, work from Chart A. Work the pattern repeat (4 sts wide) around and end with the sts after the pattern repeat. Repeat Rnds 1–2.

CABLED RIBBING B
Stitch count has to be a multiple of 4 + 2: In all rnds, work from Chart B. Work the pattern repeat (4 sts wide) around, ending with the sts after the pattern repeat. Repeat Rnds 1–2.

CABLE PATTERN
In all rnds, work from Chart C. Work the pattern repeat (36 sts wide) once in each rnd. Repeat Rnds 1–16.

Instructions

With the longest circular needle, CO 326 sts, join into round, and work 8 rnds in Hem Ribbing patt.

In the next rnd, work in pattern sequence and place markers as follows: pm, k1, pm, 30 sts Ribbing patt 1, 36 sts Cable patt, 30 sts Ribbing patt 2, pm, k1, pm, 66 sts Cabled Ribbing A, pm, k1, pm, 90 sts Ribbing patt 1, k4, pm, k1, pm, 66 sts Cabled Ribbing B.

Now, work a decrease rnd as follows: *Slip marker from left to right needle, k1, sm, sk2p, continue in pattern sequence to 2 sts before the next marker, k2tog, repeat from * 3 times more. If you do not have enough sts to comfortably fit the cable anymore, change to next shorter circular.

Repeat decreases in every 4th rnd 16 times more, then in every other rnd 11 times more—102 sts.

Divide sts onto set of US 6 (4.0 mm) DPNs and work 24 rnds in Hem Ribbing patt. Change to US 8 (5.0 mm) DPNs and work 24 rnds more in Hem Ribbing patt. BO all sts.

FINISHING
Soak the cape in lukewarm water and carefully press out excess water. Spread out on a soft surface, block to measurements, and let dry. Hide all ends.

SIZE

One size = S–L
Circumference at bust: 55 in (140 cm)
Length: 15¾ in (40 cm)

MATERIALS

#4 medium-weight yarn; shown in
Schoppel Reggae; 100% wool; 110 yd
(100 m), 1.75 oz (50 g) per skein; #581
Savannah, 12.3 oz (350 g)

US 8 (5.0 mm) circular needles, in
lengths 24 in (60 cm), 40 in (100 cm),
and 48 in (120 cm)

US 6 (4.0 mm) and US 8 (5.0 mm) sets
of DPNs

Cable needle

8 ring stitch markers

GAUGE

Stockinette st on US 8 (5.0 mm)
needles, 18 sts and 24 rows = 4 in x 4 in
(10 cm x 10 cm)

CHARTS

Page 106

RONJA

Intertwined

STOCKINETTE STITCH
Knit on RS, purl on WS.

SEED STITCH
In RS and WS rows: Alternate k1, p1, ending with k1.

Instructions

For the Back, with yarn held double, CO 118 sts and work in the following sequence: 5 sts in Seed st, 108 sts in Stockinette, 5 sts in Seed st. After 20 in (50 cm) (= 126 rows) total length, work the next RS row as follows: Break yarn, leaving a long tail, transfer 40 sts to a spare needle, with new yarn held double, BO 38 sts, hold remaining 40 sts on a second spare needle.

For the Front, with crochet hook and contrasting color waste yarn, crochet a chain of 212. From this chain, with yarn held double, pick up a total of 210 sts and work in the following sequence: 5 sts in Seed st, 200 sts in Stockinette, 5 sts in Seed st. After 20 in (50 cm) (= 126 rows) total length, leaving all sts on the needles, continue as follows: Right sides facing out, rotate Back piece and place it over the sts of the Front piece so that unworked sts are placed opposite each other, with both needle tips pointing in the same direction. Now, graft the first 40 held sts of the Back together with the opposite first 40 sts of the Front in Kitchener stitch. BO the remaining Front sts.

Pull out the provisional crochet chain at the Front, taking up the first 170 sts with the longer circular needle and the last 40 sts with the shorter circular. In a RS row, BO the 170 sts on the longer needle. Twist the Front once onto itself toward the Back, so that half of the WS of the fabric faces outward. Now, graft the remaining 40 sts of the Front together with the remaining 40 sts of the Back in Kitchener stitch (joining the WS of the Front with the RS of the Back).

FINISHING
Seam the bottom of the side edges in mattress stitch over a length of 9½ in (24 cm).
Soak the cape in lukewarm water and carefully press out excess water. Spread out on a soft surface, block to measurements, and let dry. Hide all ends.

SIZE
One size = S–L
Circumference at bust: 55 in (140 cm)

MATERIALS
#1 super fine-weight yarn; shown in Lang Yarns Baby Alpaca; 100% alpaca; 183 yd (167 m), 1.75 oz (50 g) per skein; #15 Saffron, 19.4 oz (550 g)

US 6 (4.0 mm) circular needles, in lengths 16 in (40 cm) and 48 in (120 cm)

2 spare needles
Piece of contrasting color waste yarn for provisional cast-on
US G/6 (4.0 mm) crochet hook

GAUGE
Stockinette st on US 6 (4.0 mm) needles with yarn held double, 19 sts and 25 rows = 4 in x 4 in (10 cm x 10 cm)

● ● ○

DOREEN

Naturally green

GARTER STITCH
Knit on RS and on WS.

TEXTURED PATTERN
Row 1 (WS): *Yo, slip st purlwise (yarn in back of work), k1, rep from * to end of row.

Row 2 (RS): *K1, k2tog (the yo with the slipped st of the previous row), rep from * to end of row.

Row 3: K1, *yo, slip 1 st purlwise (yarn in back of work), k1, rep from * to last st, k1.

Row 4: K2, *k2tog, k1, rep from * to end of row.
Repeat Rows 1–4.

PATTERN SEQUENCE
5 sts Garter Stitch, 100/120 sts in Textured Pattern, 5 sts Garter Stitch.

Instructions

With long circular needle, CO 110/130 sts and work 2/4 rows in Garter st. Work 1 WS row as follows: k5, 100/120 sts in Textured patt, k2, yo, k2tog, k1. The yo and the two sts knitted together form the first buttonhole. Continue in Patt Sequence, at the same time, in every following 12th row, working 8 more buttonholes as described.

At 11 in (28 cm)/11½ in (29 cm) (= 60/62 rows) total length, in the next RS row (should be in a Row 3 of Textured patt), work as follows to start shoulder decreases (changing to shorter circular as stitch count decreases): k5, 10 sts in Textured patt, *k3tog, 13 sts in Textured patt, repeat from * 4/5 times more, ending with k3tog, 7/11 sts in Textured patt, k5—98/116 sts.

Work 7 rows in Patt Sequence, then work 1 decrease rnd as follows: k5, 8/6 sts in Textured patt, *k3tog, 5/7 sts in Textured Patt, repeat from * 9 times more, k5—78/96 sts.

Work 7 rows in Patt Sequence, then work 1 decrease rnd as follows: k5, 4/6 sts in Textured patt, *k3tog, 11/7 sts in Textured patt, repeat from * 3/7 times more, ending with k3tog/k0tog, 5/0 sts in Textured patt, k5—68/80 sts.

SIZES
S/M and L/XL

Numbers for size S/M are listed before the slash, for size L/XL after the slash. If only one number is given, it applies to both sizes.

Circumference at bust: 43¼ in (110 cm)/51¼ in (130 cm)

Length: 15 in (38 cm)/15½ in (39 cm)

MATERIALS
#5 bulky-weight yarn; shown in Schachenmayr Merino Extrafine 40; 100% wool; 43.7 yd (40 m), 1.75 oz (50 g) per skein; #373 Apple, 15.9 oz (450 g)/21.2 oz (600 g)

US 10¾ (7.0 mm) circular knitting needles, in lengths 16 in (40 cm) and 40 in (100 cm)

9 buttons in green, approx. 1 in (24 mm)

GAUGE
Textured patt on US 10¾ (7.0 mm) needles, 10 sts and 21 rows = 4 in x 4 in (10 cm x 10 cm)

● ● ○

Work 7 rows in Patt Sequence, then work 1 decrease rnd as follows: k5, 4/2 sts in Textured patt, *k3tog, 5 sts in Textured patt, repeat from * 5/7 times more, ending with k3tog, 3/1 sts in Textured patt, k5—54/62 sts.

Work 3 rows in Patt Sequence, then work last decrease row as follows: k5, 6/4 sts in Textured patt, *k3tog, 3/5 sts in Textured patt, repeat from * 5 times more, ending with 2/0 sts in Textured patt, k5—42/50 sts.

Work another 11 rows in Patt Sequence, then 2 rows Garter st, and BO all sts.

FINISHING

Soak the cape in lukewarm water and carefully press out excess water. Spread out on a soft surface, block to measurements, and let dry. Hide all ends. Sew the buttons to the Garter Stitch button band according to the position of the buttonholes, then button the cape.

RAQUEL

Classically classy

STOCKINETTE STITCH
Knit on RS, purl on WS.

GARTER STITCH
Knit on RS and on WS.

SIZE
One size = S–L
Circumference at bust: 55 in (140 cm)

MATERIALS
#3 light-weight chainette yarn in 2 colors; shown in Lang Yarns Novena; 50% merino wool, 30% alpaca, 20% nylon; 120.3 yd (110 m), 0.9 oz (25 g) per skein; A: #05 Grey, 8.8 oz (250 g), and B: #04 Black, 0.9 oz (25 g)

US 7 (4.5 mm) circular knitting needles, in lengths 16 in (40 cm), 32 in (80 cm), and 48 in (120 cm)

3 ring stitch markers

2 buttons in black, approx. 1 in (25 mm)

Garment closure (hook and eye) in black

GAUGE
Stockinette st on US 7 (4.5 mm) needles, 16 sts and 28 rows = 4 in x 4 in (10 cm x 10 cm)

Instructions

With short circular needle and B, CO 109 sts and work 4 rows in Garter st. Break yarn, leaving a long tail, and continue with A in Stockinette. Purl 1 WS row (this row is not included in the following row counts), then continue as follows:

Row 1: K1, M1L, *k26, M1R, pm, slip 1 st purlwise with yarn in back, M1L, rep from * 2 times more, k26, M1R, k1.

Row 2: Purl all sts, slipping markers from left to right needle as you encounter them.

Row 3: *Knit to next marker, sm, slip 1 st purlwise with yarn in back, rep from * 2 times more, knit to end of row.

Row 4: Work the same as Row 2.

Row 5: K1, M1L, *knit to next marker, M1R, sm, slip 1 st purlwise with yarn in back, M1L, rep from * 2 times more, knit to last st, M1R, k1.

Row 6: Work the same as Row 2.

Repeat Rows 3–6; there will be 8 increases each in every fourth row.

At the same time, in Rows 11 and 27 from CO (always in a non-increase row), work buttonholes as follows: As described in Row 3, work to last 8 sts of row, BO 2 sts, k5. In the next WS row, CO 2 new sts over the 2 bound-off sts.

After having worked 20 in (50.5 cm) (= 142 rows) in A, there will be 397 sts on the needles. Break yarn, leaving a long tail, and in B work another 4 rows Garter st, then BO all sts.

With B, pick up and knit 102 sts each from the front edges and work 4 rows in Garter st. BO all sts.

FINISHING

Soak the cape in lukewarm water and carefully press out excess water. Spread out on a soft surface, block to measurements, and let dry. Hide all ends.

Sew the first button to the left front at the height of the top buttonhole 6 in (15 cm) in from the edge, the second button in height of the bottom buttonhole 5½ in (14 cm) in from the edge.

Sew the eye part of the garment closure to the left front at the very edge of the neckline, and the corresponding hook to the right front at the inner edge of the neckline approx. 6¾ in (17 cm) in from the edge.

HELENA

Simply beautiful

STOCKINETTE STITCH
In rounds: Knit all sts in all rounds.

GARTER STITCH
In rounds: Alternate knit 1 rnd, purl 1 rnd.

BOBBLE
Work [k1, p1, k1] into the same stitch, turn work and [p1, k1, p1], turn work again [k1, p1, k1], then one after another pass the 2nd and 3rd st over the 1st one and off the needle.

LACE PATTERN 1
Work from Chart A. Only odd-numbered rounds are shown; in even-numbered rnds, work all sts as they appear (knit the knits and purl the purls), knit all yo's. Work the pattern repeat (10 sts wide) 8 times in each rnd, working Rounds 1–8 once.

LACE PATTERN 2
Work from Chart B. Only RS rows are shown; in WS rows, purl all sts and yo's. Work the pattern once, repeating Rows 1–12.

Instructions

With DPNs, CO 80 sts, evenly distribute onto DPNs, and join into round.

Work 1 rnd as follows: k5, *bobble, k4, repeat from * 14 times more. After this, work 8 rnds in Lace patt 1 from Chart A, then 4 rnds in Garter st.

Change to short circular needle and continue in Stockinette starting increases in Rnd 1 right away as follows: *k4, M1R, repeat from * 19 times more—100 sts.

Knit 1 rnd, then work next increases as follows: *k5, M1R, repeat from * 19 times more—120 sts.

Continue as follows:

Work 5 rnds in Stockinette.

Next inc rnd: *K3, M1R, repeat from * 39 times more—160 sts.

SIZE
One size = S–L
Circumference at bust: 57 in (145 cm)

MATERIALS
#0 lace-weight mohair/wool yarn; shown in Rowan Mohair Haze; 70% mohair, 30% wool; 111.6 yd (102 m), 0.9 oz (25 g) per skein; #532 True, 4.4 oz (125 g)

US 4 (3.5 mm) circular knitting needles, in lengths 16 in (40 cm), 32 in (80 cm), and 48 in (120 cm)

US 2 or 3 (3.0 mm) set of DPNs or short straight needles

US C or D (3.0 mm) crochet hook

Piece of waste yarn in contrasting color for provisional cast-on

Spare needle

GAUGE
Stockinette st on US 4 (3.5 mm) needles,
22 sts and 26 rows = 4 in x 4 in (10 cm x 10 cm)

CHARTS
Page 104

Work 5 rnds in Stockinette.

Next inc rnd: *K4, M1R, repeat from * 39 times more—200 sts.

Work 7 rnds in Stockinette.

Next inc rnd: *K5, M1R, repeat from * 39 times more—240 sts.

Work 7 rnds in Stockinette.

Next inc rnd: *K6, M1R, repeat from * 39 times more—280 sts.

Work 5 rnds in Stockinette.

Next inc rnd: *K7, M1R, repeat from * 39 times more—320 sts.

Work 2 rnds in Stockinette.

Next inc rnd: *K80, M1R, repeat from * 3 times more—324 sts.

Work another 34 rnds in Stockinette and 4 rnds in Garter st without increases. Leave all sts on the needles.

For the lace edging, with crochet hook and waste yarn in contrasting color, crochet a chain of about 12. Then, using 2 DPNs or a short circular, continue as follows: Pick up 9 sts from the crocheted chain, then purl 1 WS row. Now, work in Lace patt 2 from Chart B, and in every RS row, k2tog the last edging st with the next st of the body of the cape. After all sts of the body of the cape have been used up, carefully pull out the crocheted chain, taking up the freed sts with a spare needle. Graft the live sts of the opposite edges in Kitchener stitch.

FINISHING

Soak the cape in lukewarm water and carefully press out excess water. Spread out on a soft surface and block to measurements, slightly pulling out the points of the lace edging. Let dry and hide all ends.

ILKA

Gently rolling waves

SEED STITCH FOR EVEN STITCH COUNT

In RS rows: Alternate k1, p1.
In WS rows: Alternate p1, k1.

SEED STITCH FOR ODD STITCH COUNT

In RS and WS rows: Alternate k1, p1, ending with k1.

RIBBING PATTERN

Alternate k2, p2.

WAVE PATTERN

Stitch count has to be a multiple of 7 + 4. Work from Charts A and B. Only RS rows are shown; in WS rows, purl all sts. Begin with the sts before the pattern repeat, repeat the pattern repeat (8 sts wide, with gray background), ending with the sts after the pattern repeat. Repeat Rows 1–24 of the charts all the time.

Instructions

With circular needle, CO 162 sts, and for bottom edging, work 6 rows in Seed st. After this, work 1 RS row in the following pattern sequence: 3 sts Seed st, 74 sts Wave patt from Chart A, k1, M1R, place marker, 6 sts Seed st, pm, M1L, k1, 74 sts Wave patt from Chart B, 3 sts Seed st—164 sts. In WS rows, purl the newly created sts; in every row, slip markers from left to right needle.

SIZE

One size = S–XL
Measurements: 40 in x 23 in (100 cm x 58 cm)

MATERIALS

#3 light-weight wool/cotton yarn; shown in Schachenmayr Merino Extrafine Cotton 120; 50% wool, 50% cotton; 131.2 yd (120 m), 1.75 oz (50 g) per skein; #571 Sea Green, 19.4 oz (550 g)
US 4 (3.5 mm) circular knitting needle, 48 in (120 cm) long

US 2.5 (3.0 mm) set of DPNs
2 ring stitch markers
2 spare needles

GAUGE

Wave patt from Chart A on US 4 (3.5 mm) needles, 22 sts and 30 rows = 4 in x 4 in (10 cm x 10 cm)

CHARTS

Page 108

Continue in this manner, increasing 2 sts each in every RS row as follows: Work in pattern sequence to 1 st before the first marker, M1R, k1, sm, 6 sts Seed st, sm, k1, M1L, work in pattern sequence to end of row. Always incorporate the 2 newly added sts into the Wave patt, making sure that increases and decreases cancel each other out.

After 12½ in (32 cm) (= 96 rows or 4 pattern repeats heightwise) from the Seed st edge, there are 258 sts on the needles. In the next RS row, continue for the neckline in the following manner: 3 sts Seed st, work in Wave patt from Chart A to 1 st before the first marker, M1R, k1, sm, 3 sts Seed st. Always incorporate the newly added st into the Wave patt. Transfer remaining 129 sts to a spare needle for holding. Now, for the right side, first work 96 rows (= 4 pattern repeats heightwise) even in this manner (no more increases are worked). In Row 95 (RS) from division, decrease the gained sts again as follows: Work in pattern sequence to 2 sts before the marker, k2tog, sm, 3 sts in Seed Stitch.

Place all sts on a spare needle for holding and work the left half mirror-inverted. For this, take up the formerly held sts again with a circular and work as follows: 3 sts in Seed st, sm, k1, M1R, work in Wave patt from Chart B to last 3 sts of row, 3 sts in Seed st. Always incorporate the gained st into the Wave patt in subsequent rows. In Row 95 (RS) from separation, decrease the gained sts again as follows: 3 sts Seed st, sm, sk2p, continue in pattern sequence to end of row.

After 12½ in (32 cm) (= 96 rows or 4 pattern repeats heightwise) from division, take up the formerly held sts of the right half again with a circular and continue over all 258 sts in pattern sequence as done before the division for the neckline. At the same time, in every RS row, work 2 decreases each as follows: Work in pattern sequence to 2 sts before the first marker, k2tog, sm, 6 sts in Seed st, sm, sk2p, work in pattern sequence to end of row. Here, too, match the Wave patt to the decreases, and make sure increases and decreases cancel each other out.

After 12½ in (32 cm) (= 96 rows or 4 pattern repeats heightwise) from end of neckline, there will again be 162 sts on the needles. Work another 6 rows in Seed st, then BO all sts.

For the mock turtleneck, with DPN set and RS of fabric facing out, pick up and knit 136 sts around the neckline edge, and evenly distribute onto 4 DPNs. Work Ribbing patt in the round for 4 in (10 cm) (= 30 rows), then BO all sts.

FINISHING

Soak the cape in lukewarm water and carefully press out excess water. Spread out on a soft surface, block to measurements, and let dry. Hide all ends.

SIZES

S–L and XL–XXL

Numbers for size S–L are listed before the slash, for size XL–XXL after the slash. If only one number is given, it applies to both sizes.

Height: 21¾ in (55 cm)

Width: 48 in (120 cm)

Upper arm width: 11¾ in (30 cm)/13¾ in (35 cm)

MATERIALS

#3 light-weight yarn; shown in Lang Yarns Merino 120; 100% wool; 131 yd (120 m), 1.75 oz (50 g) per skein; #86 Fire, 31.8 oz (900 g)

US 6 (4.0 mm) circular needle, 48 in (120 cm) long

Cable needle or spare needle

Removable marker

GAUGE

Seed st on US 6 (4.0 mm) needles, 22 sts and 32 rows = 4 x 4 in (10 cm x 10 cm)

CHART

Page 107

● ● ○

OPHELIA

Stop-light red

SELVEDGE STITCHES
In RS rows: Knit the selv sts.
In WS rows: Purl the selv sts.

RIBBING PATTERN
RS: Alternate k1, p1.
WS: Work all sts as they appear (knit the knits and purl the purls).

SEED STITCH
In RS rows: Alternate k1, p1.
In WS rows: Alternate p1, k1.

CABLE PATTERN
Work from chart. Only RS rows are shown; in WS rows, work as explained in knitting symbol legend. Start with the sts before the pattern repeat, work the pattern repeat (34 sts wide) 7 times, and end with the st after the pattern repeat. Work Rows 1–48 a total of 3 times, then repeat only Rows 1–6 once more.

Tip: Using stitch markers to separate the pattern panels will make it easier to keep track of where you are in the pattern.

Instructions

FRONT
CO 262 sts and work 1½ in (4 cm) (= 14 rows) in Ribbing patt, then continue as follows: 10 sts in Ribbing patt, 242 sts in Cable patt from chart, 10 sts in Ribbing patt.
After 18½ in (47 cm) (= 150 rows) in Cable patt, work another 1½ in (4 cm) (= 14 rows) in Ribbing patt. In the next RS row, BO the middle 58 sts for the neckline, work to the end of the row, and place a marker (= end of Front). Break yarn, leaving a long tail.

BACK
Slide the sts on the circular needle so that you will be able to work a RS row in Ribbing patt again. In this RS row, CO 58 new sts over the formerly bound off 58 sts, and continue to the end of the row. Work 1½ in (4 cm) (= 13 rows) more in Ribbing patt, then work in the same panel sequence as for the Front. After 18½ in (47 cm) (= 150 rows) in Cable patt, work another 1½ in (4 cm) (= 14 rows) in Ribbing patt, then BO all sts.

SLEEVES (MAKE 2)
CO 46/56 sts and work 1¼ in (3 cm) (= 10 rows) in Ribbing patt. Now, work in Seed st. For sleeve tapering, after 4 rows Seed st, on both sides increase 1 st each. Repeat this increase in every 4th row 9/10 times more—66/78 sts. After 5¼ in (13.5 cm)/6 in (15 cm) (= 44/48 rows) in Seed st, BO all sts.

FINISHING
Soak all pieces in lukewarm water and carefully press out excess water. Spread out on a soft surface, block to measurements, and let dry. Close side seams in mattress stitch, leaving open 6 in (15 cm)/7 in (17.5 cm) at the top for armholes. Sew in the sleeves and close sleeve seams. Hide all ends.

LISSI
Like gently melting caramel

STOCKINETTE STITCH
In rows: Knit on RS, purl on WS.
In rounds: Knit all sts in all rounds.

GARTER STITCH
In rows: Knit on RS and on WS.
In rounds: Alternate knit 1 rnd, purl 1 rnd.

CABLE PATTERN IN ROWS
Work from Chart A. Only RS rows are shown; in WS rows, work all sts as they appear (knit the knits and purl the purls), purl all slipped sts. Work the pattern repeat (21 sts wide) once, repeating Rows 1–8 all the time.

CABLE PATTERN IN ROUNDS
In all rnds, work from Chart B. Work the pattern repeat (21 sts wide) once, repeating Rounds 1–8 all the time.

ACCENTED DECREASES
At the beginning of the row: K1, sk2p.
At the end of the row: K2tog, k1.

Instructions

BACK
With long circular needle, CO 127 sts and for the edging, work 10 rows as follows: 53 sts in Garter st, 21 sts in Cable patt from Chart A, 53 sts in Garter st. After this, continue over the 53 sts before and after the Cable patt in Stockinette, continuing the Cable patt.
At 60 rows from edging, for shaping at both sides, work 1 Accented Decrease, then, in every other row, work Accented Decreases on both sides 18 times more. After this, on both sides, BO 2 sts 2 times, 4 sts 4 times, and 5 sts once. After 112 rows from edging, transfer remaining 39 sts to a spare needle for holding.

FRONT
Work the same as the Back, but include sleeve slits and neck opening. After 30 rows from edging, continue for the bottom slit edging of the armholes in the following manner: 18 sts in Stockinette, 17 sts in Garter st, 18 sts in Stockinette, 21 sts in Cable patt from Chart A, 18 sts Stockinette, 17 sts Garter st, 18 sts

SIZE
One size = S–XL
Circumference at bust: 59 in (150 cm)
Height: 25½ in (65 cm)

MATERIALS
#2 fine-weight mohair/silk yarn; shown in Lang Yarns Mohair Trend; 70% mohair, 30% silk; 82 yd (75 m), 0.9 oz (25 g) per skein; #96 Beige, 10.6 oz (300 g)

US 8 (5.0 mm) circular needles, in lengths 16 in (40 cm) and 40 in (100 cm)

3 spare needles

GAUGE
Stockinette st on US 8 (5.0 mm) needles, 14 sts and 20 rows = 4 in x 4 in (10 cm x 10 cm)

CHARTS
Page 106

Stockinette. After 10 rows in this manner, BO the 17 Garter sts for each of the armhole slit edgings. In the next WS row, CO new sts over the previously bound-off sts. After this, for the top slit edging, work an additional 10 rows in the same way as for the bottom slit edging. Resume to work over all sts before and after the cable section again in Stockinette.

Work shaping decreases the same way as for the Back. At the same time, for the neckline, after 106 rows from edging, BO the middle 23 sts and continue both sides separately. For neckline shaping, at the inner (neckside) edge in every other row, on both sides, BO 2 sts once and 1 st once. After 112 rows from edging, BO remaining 5 sts on each side.

FINISHING

Close side and shoulder seams. For the hood, with short circular needle, pick up and knit a total of 61 sts as follows: Beginning left of the 9 middle sts of the front neckline, pick up and knit 11 sts to the beginning of the held Back sts, the 39 formerly held Back sts, then after the end of the cable pattern, at right of the 9 middle sts of the front neckline, again 11 sts. Work 1 WS row as follows: p20, 21 sts in Cable patt from Chart A, p20.

Beginning with the next RS row, work short rows as follows:

Rows 1–2: K5, turn work, yo, p5.
Rows 3–4: K10 (k2tog the yo of the previous row with the next st), turn work, yo, p10.
Rows 5–6: K15 (k2tog the yo of the previous row with the next st), turn work, yo, p15.
Rows 7–8: K20 (k2tog the yo of the previous row with the next st), turn work, yo, p20.

In the next row, work as follows: K20, 21 sts Cable patt (slipping the 1st st of the cable pattern together with the yo), k20.

From the next WS row, work short rows again as follows:

Rows 1–2: P5, turn work, yo, k5.
Rows 3–4: P10 (p2tog the yo of the previous row with the next st), turn work, yo, k10.
Rows 5–6: P15 (p2tog the yo of the previous row with the next st), turn work, yo, k15.
Rows 7–8: P20 (p2tog the yo of the previous row with the next st), turn work, yo, k20.

In the next row, work as follows: P20, 21 sts Cable patt (p2tog the 1st and 21st st of the cable pattern with the yo), p20.

Now, work 30 rows in the following sequence: 20 sts in Stockinette, 21 sts in Cable patt, 20 sts in Stockinette. After this, work hood shaping decreases as follows: Knit to 2 sts before beginning of Cable patt, ssk, 21 sts Cable patt, k2tog, knit to end of row. Repeat these decreases in every other row 4 times more—51 sts.

Now, transfer the first and the last 15 sts to a spare needle each, with the needle tips pointing toward the cable section. Continue over the remaining 21 sts in Cable patt, while in every RS row, ssk the last st of the Cable patt with the first st from the spare needle, turn work, and in WS rows, p2tog the last st of the Cable patt with the first st from the spare needle, then turn work again. Repeat these decreases until all sts from the spare needles have been used up. Transfer the remaining 21 sts to a spare needle for holding.

For the hood edging, starting at the first of the 9 middle sts of the front neckline, pick up and knit 47 sts to the beginning of the held sts, continue over the 21 held sts in Cable patt, then pick up and knit 38 sts from the right edge of the hood—106 sts. Now, continue in rnds as follows: 47 sts Garter st, 21 sts Cable patt from Chart B, 38 sts Garter st. After 8 rnds in this manner, BO all sts.

Soak the cape in lukewarm water and gently
squeeze out excess water. Spread out on a
soft surface, block to measurements, and let
dry. Hide all ends.

JAINA

Float on clouds

STOCKINETTE STITCH
Knit on RS, purl on WS.

GARTER STITCH
Knit on RS and on WS.

TEXTURED PATTERN
Row 1: Selv st, knit to last st, selv st.
Row 2: Selv st, *k2tog, rep from * to last st, selv st.
Row 3: Selv st, *kfb, rep from * to last st, selv st.
Row 4: Selv st, purl to last st, selv st.
Repeat Rows 1–4 all the time.

SELVEDGE STITCHES
Knit the selvedge sts on RS and WS.

LACE PATTERN
Work from Chart A. Only RS rows are shown; in WS rows, purl all sts and yo's. Start with the sts before the pattern repeat, work the pattern repeat (10 sts wide) 28 times, end with the sts after the pattern repeat. Work Rows 1–16 of the chart once.

CABLE PATTERN
Work from Chart B. Only RS rows are shown; in WS rows, work all sts as they appear (knit the knits and purl the purls). Work the pattern repeat (16 sts wide) 18 times. Work Rows 1–24 twice, then repeat only Rows 1–22 once.

Instructions

For the lace edging, with US 2.5 (3.0 mm) circular knitting needle and yarn B, CO 293 sts and work as follows: selv st, 291 sts Lace patt from Chart A, selv st. After 16 rows Lace patt, change to US 4 (3.5 mm) circular needle and work 12 rows Stockinette; in the last row, decrease 3 sts evenly distributed—290 sts. Place all sts on a spare needle for holding.

For the cape, with long US 6 (4.0 mm) circular needle and yarn A, CO 290 sts and work 4 rows Garter st. Now, work 11 rows in Textured patt, first working Rows 1–4 of the Textured patt twice, then repeating only Rows 1–3 once.

SIZE
One size = S–XL
Circumference at bust: 55 in (140 cm)

MATERIALS
A: #3 light-weight yarn; shown in Lang Yarns Merino 120; 100% wool; 131 yd (120 m), 1.75 oz (50 g) per skein; #21 Light Blue, 14.1 oz (400 g)

B: #0 lace-weight yarn; shown in Lang Yarns Merino 400 Lace; 219 yd (200 m), 0.9 oz (25 g) per skein; #94 White, 0.9 oz (25 g)

US 6 (4.0 mm) circular needles, in lengths 24 in (60 cm), 40 in (100 cm), and 63 in (160 cm)

US 2.5 (3.0 mm) circular knitting needle, 63 in (160 cm) long

US 4 (3.5 mm) circular knitting needle, 63 in (160 cm) long

Cable needle

Spare needle

9 half-ball buttons, approx. ½ in (12 mm)

GAUGE
Textured patt on US 6 (4.0 mm) needles with yarn A, 20 sts and 32 rows = 4 x 4 in (10 cm x 10 cm)

CHARTS
Page 107

•••

Knit 1 WS row, then continue as follows: Hold the lace edging on the spare needle behind the cape sts on the circular needle. Now, in A, k2tog, always 1 cape st with 1 st of the lace edging (white) until all sts of the lace edging have been used up. Continue in A and work 4 rows Garter st, then continue as follows: 2 selv sts, 288 sts Cable patt from Chart B, 2 selv sts. After 70 rows of Cable patt, work another 4 rows in Garter st. Continue in Textured patt, starting decreases immediately in Row 1 as follows (changing to next shorter circular as stitch count decreases): *k27, k2tog, repeat from * 9 times more —280 sts.

3 rows in Textured patt, then work 2nd dec row: *k5, k2tog, repeat from * 39 times more— 240 sts.

3 rows in Textured patt, then work 3rd dec row: *k4, k2tog, repeat from * 39 times more— 200 sts.

7 rows in Textured patt, then work 4th dec row: *k3, k2tog, repeat from * 39 times more— 160 sts.

7 rows in Textured patt, then work 5th dec row: *k6, k2tog, repeat from * 19 times more— 140 sts.

7 rows in Textured patt, then work 6th dec row: *k5, k2tog, repeat from * 19 times more— 120 sts.

6 rows in Textured patt, then knit 1 WS row and BO all sts.

For the buttonhole band, with medium-length US 6 (4.0 mmm) circular needle and yarn A, RS facing out, pick up and knit 67 sts along the right front edge and work 2 rows Garter st. In the next row, work 9 buttonholes as follows: k3, *yo, k2tog, k5, repeat from * 7 times more, then yo, k2tog, k6. Work another 4 rows Garter st, then BO all sts loosely.

For the button band, likewise pick up and knit 67 sts along the left front edge, and work 7 rows Garter st. Bind off all sts loosely.

FINISHING

Soak the cape in lukewarm water and carefully press out excess water. Spread out on a soft surface, block to measurements, and let dry. Slightly pull out the points of the lace edging. Hide all ends. Sew buttons onto button band according to buttonhole placement.

NADIA
Snuggle-worthy

STOCKINETTE STITCH
Knit on RS, purl on WS.

GARTER STITCH
Knit on both RS and WS.

RIBBING PATTERN FOR EVEN STITCH COUNT
In RS rows: Alternate k1, p1.
In WS rows: Work all sts as they appear (knit the knits and purl the purls).

RIBBING PATTERN FOR ODD STITCH COUNT
In RS rows: Alternate k1, p1, ending with k1.
In WS rows: Work all sts as they appear (knit the knits and purl the purls).

NORWEGIAN COLORWORK MOTIFS
In RS and WS rows: work in Stockinette according to Colorwork Chart on page 103. When changing colors, cross strands in back of work to avoid holes. Repeat the pattern repeat (27 sts wide) widthwise. Work Rows 1–31 once.

CABLE PATTERN
Work from chart on page 104. Only RS rows are shown; in WS rows, purl all sts. Start with the stitch before the pattern repeat, repeat the pattern repeat (6 sts wide) widthwise, and end with the stitch after the pattern repeat. Repeat Rows 1–8.

SIZE
One size = S–XXL
Width: 49¼ in (125 cm)
Height: 27 in (68 cm)

MATERIALS
#4 medium-weight yarn in 3 colors; shown in Lang Yarns Carpe Diem; 70% merino wool, 30% alpaca; 98.5 yd (90 m), 1.75 oz (50 g) per skein; A: #26 Nature, 23 oz (650 g), B: #148 Dusty Pink, 5.3 oz (150 g), and C: #368 Brown, 8.8 oz (250 g)

US 9 (5.5 mm) circular knitting needle, 48 in (120 cm) long

Cable needle
Spare needle
Removable marker

GAUGE
Stockinette st on US 9 (5.5 mm) needles, 16 sts and 22 rows = 4 in x 4 in (10 cm x 10 cm)

PATTERN CHART
Page 104

COLORWORK CHART
Page 103

● ● ●

Instructions

In C, CO 203 sts and work 12 rows in Ribbing patt, then continue as follows:

2 rows in C: 7 sts in Ribbing patt, 189 sts in Stockinette, 7 sts Ribbing patt.

2 rows in B: 7 sts in Ribbing patt, 189 sts Garter st, 7 sts in Ribbing patt.

31 rows in Norwegian Colorwork Motifs: 7 sts in Ribbing patt in C, 189 sts in Norwegian Colorwork Motifs, 7 sts in Ribbing patt in C.

Break working yarn and slide the sts to the other end of the needle to again begin a RS row next.

2 rows in B: 7 sts in Ribbing patt, 189 sts Garter st, 7 sts in Ribbing patt while decreasing 1 st in Row 1—202 sts.

Break the yarns, leaving long ends, and slide the sts to the other end of the circular needle to again begin a RS row next.

Now, continue in A in the following manner: 7 sts in Ribbing patt, 188 sts in Cable patt, 7 sts in Ribbing patt.

After 16¾ in (42.5 cm) (= 94 rows) in Cable patt, continue as follows: 7 sts in Ribbing patt, 80 sts in Cable patt (working the last 3 sts as k3), 28 sts in Ribbing patt, 80 sts in Cable patt, 7 sts in Ribbing patt. Work another 7 rows in this manner, then continue for the back neckline as follows: 7 sts in Ribbing patt, 80 sts Cable patt, 7 sts in Ribbing patt, BO 15 sts, transfer remaining 93 sts to a spare needle for holding.

For the right front, work an additional WS row in the established pattern over the first 94 sts. Mark this row (shoulder line). Continue in established pattern.

After 18½ in (47 cm) (= 104 rows) from shoulder line, continue as follows:

2 rows in B: 7 sts in Ribbing patt, 80 sts Garter st, 7 sts Ribbing, while in the last row increasing 1 st—95 sts.

31 rows Norwegian Colorwork Motifs: 7 sts Ribbing patt in C, 81 sts Norwegian Colorwork Motifs, 7 sts Ribbing patt in C.

Break working yarn and slide the sts to the other end of the needle to again begin a RS row next.

2 rows in B: 7 sts in Ribbing patt, 81 sts Garter st, 7 sts in Ribbing patt.

2 rows in C: 7 sts in Ribbing patt, 81 sts in Stockinette, 7 sts in Ribbing patt.

12 rows in C: 95 sts in Ribbing patt.

BO all sts.

With circular needle, take up the formerly held sts again and work the left front the same as the right front, working the first row as follows: 6 sts in Ribbing patt, M1R, 80 sts in Cable patt, 7 sts in Ribbing patt—94 sts. Work over all sts again as done for the right front, taking care that Cable patt's align.

FINISHING

Soak the cape in lukewarm water, carefully press out excess water, and place on a soft surface for blocking. Graft the bottom of the side edges in Kitchener stitch over a height of 11¾ in (30 cm). Hide all ends.

LUNA

Truly perfect

STOCKINETTE STITCH

In rows: Knit on RS, purl on WS.
In rounds: Knit all sts in all rounds.

SELVEDGE STITCHES

Work selv sts in Stockinette.

FAIR ISLE PATTERN

Work all rnds in Stockinette according to Colorwork Chart. Work the pattern repeat (10 sts wide) widthwise, ending with the st after the pattern repeat. Repeat Rows 1–60.

RIBBING PATTERN

Alternate k1, p1.

Instructions

With long circular needle and A, CO 322 sts, join into round, and for the edging, work 1 in (2.5 cm) (= 6 rows) in Ribbing patt, then continue in the following manner: *161 sts in Stockinette in Fair Isle patt from Colorwork Chart (work pattern repeat 16 times, place marker, k1 after the pattern repeat, place marker), repeat from * once. The 2 sts between stitch markers form the imagined side seam. Continue in this way.

After 5 rnds from ribbed edge, work 4 side-shaping decreases as follows: *Work in pattern sequence to 2 sts before the first marker, k2tog, sm, k1 from Colorwork Chart, sm, sk2p, repeat from * once, matching the Fair Isle patt to the decreases. Repeat decreases in every 6th rnd 6 times more— 294 sts.

After 9½ in (24 cm) (= 62 rnds) from ribbed edge, work is divided into Back and Front to be continued separately in back-and-forth rows.

BACK

For the armholes, first BO 5 sts, then work in Fair Isle patt from Colorwork Chart to 1 st before the first marker, slip 1 st purlwise, remove marker, pass the slipped st back to the left needle and knit it together with the side

SIZE

One size = S–L
Circumference at bust: 55 in (140 cm)

MATERIALS

#3 light-weight yarn in 7 colors; shown in Schachenmayr Wool 125; 100% superwash wool; 137 yd (125 m), 1.75 oz (50 g) per skein; A: #198 Anthracite, 7 oz (200 g), B: #121 Golden, 3.5 oz (100 g), C: #178 Grass, 3.5 oz (100 g), D: #171 Olive, 1.75 oz (50 g), E: #195 Stone, 1.75 oz (50 g), F: #169 Petrol, 1.75 oz (50 g), and G: #132 Burgundy, 1.75 oz (50 g)

US 4 (3.5 mm) circular knitting needles, in lengths 16 in (40 cm), 32 in (80 cm), and 48 in (120 cm)

US 4 (3.5 mm) set of DPNs

4 removable stitch markers

Spare needle

GAUGE

Stockinette st in Fair Isle patt with US 5 (3.5 mm) needles, 22 sts and 26 rows = 4 in x 4 in (10 cm x 10 cm)

COLORWORK CHART

Page 102

seam st, remove the second marker. Transfer the remaining sts, including the two remaining markers, to a spare needle for holding. There are now 141 sts on the needles, and you will continue with a shorter circular in back-and-forth rows. In the next WS row, BO the first 5 sts for the second armhole, and over the remaining 136 sts, work another 22 rows in Fair Isle patt according to Colorwork Chart. In the next RS row, continue side-shaping decreases at the right and left edge of the piece as follows: selv st, sk2p, work in Stockinette in Fair Isle patt from Colorwork Chart to last 3 sts of row, k2tog, selv st. Repeat these decreases in every 6th row 7 times more—120 sts.

After 17¼ in (44 cm) (= 114 rows) from ribbed edge, for shoulder sloping BO 2 sts each on both sides once, then BO 2 sts each on both sides each in every other row, 17 times more. After 22½ in (57.5 cm) (= 150 rows) from ribbed edge, BO remaining 48 sts.

FRONT

With circular needle, take up the formerly held sts again. Work the front the same as the back, but with neckline. For this, after 20 in (51 cm) (= 134 rows) from ribbed edge, BO middle 18 sts and continue both sides separately. For neckline shaping, BO sts at the inner (neckside) edge in every other row as follows: BO 3 sts twice, 2 sts twice, and 1 st 3 times. Now, BO last 2 sts. At the same time, continue shoulder-sloping decreases as described for the Back.

FINISHING

Close shoulder seams. With 3 DPNs and A, pick up and knit 88 sts each around armhole edges, distribute sts evenly onto 3 DPNs, and join into round. Work 6 rnds in Ribbing patt,

then BO all sts. Around the neckline, using short circular needle and A, pick up and knit 98 sts and work 6 rnds in Ribbing patt. BO all sts.

Soak in lukewarm water and carefully press out excess water. Spread out on a soft surface, block to measurements, and let dry. Hide all ends.

SMILLA
Patterned to advantage

STOCKINETTE STITCH
Knit on RS, purl on WS.

DOUBLE SEED STITCH
Row 1: *K1, p1, rep from * to last st, k1.
Row 2: Knit the knits and purl the purls.
Row 3: *P1, k1, rep from * to last st, p1.
Row 4: Knit the knits and purl the purls.
Repeat Rows 1–4.

FAIR ISLE PATTERN
Work all rows in Stockinette from Colorwork Charts A–C. Repeat the pattern repeat (always 18 sts wide) and end with the st after the pattern repeat. Repeat Rows 1–18.

CABLE PATTERN
Work from Charts 1 and 2. Only RS rows are shown; in WS rows, work all sts as they appear (knit the knits and purl the purls). Work the pattern repeat (8 sts wide) once widthwise. Repeat Rows 1–4.

RIBBING PATTERN
Alternate k1, p1.

SIZE
One size = S–XXL
Width: 49¼ in (125 cm)
Height: 30 in (75 cm)

MATERIALS
#4 medium-weight yarn in 4 colors; shown in Lang Yarns Cashsoft; 50% cashmere, 50% merino wool; 120.3 yd (110 m), 1.75 oz (50 g) per skein; A: #33 Denim Blue, 19.4 oz (550 g), B: #70 Anthracite, 10.6 oz (300 g), C: #03 Light Grey, 5.3 oz (150 g), and D: #05 Medium Grey, 3.5 oz (100 g)

US 8 (5.0 mm) circular needles, in lengths 16 in (40 cm) and 48 in (120 cm)

6 buttons, approx. 1 in (22 mm)

GAUGE
Stockinette st in Fair Isle patt on US 8 (5.0 mm) needles, 18 sts and 21 rows = 4 in x 4 in (10 cm x 10 cm)

PATTERN CHARTS
Page 104

COLORWORK CHARTS
Page 103

● ● ●

Instructions

BACK

With long circular needle and A, CO 211 sts and work 11 rows in Double Seed st. Work a WS row as follows: p73, k2, p4, k2, 49 sts in Double Seed st, k2, p4, k2, p73.

Now, work 18 rows in the following pattern sequence: 73 sts in Fair Isle patt from Colorwork Chart A, 8 sts in Cable patt from Chart 1, 49 sts in Double Seed st, 8 sts in Cable patt from Chart 2, 73 sts in Fair Isle patt from Colorwork Chart A—211 sts.

After this, work an additional 18 rows in this pattern sequence, this time from Colorwork Chart B (instead of A), then again 32 rows from Colorwork Chart A.

Finally, work in the same pattern sequence, but this time from Colorwork Chart C (instead of A). At 26¼ in (66.5 cm) (= 140 rows) total length, for shoulder sloping, on both sides, BO 9 sts once, then BO 8 sts each in every other row on both sides, 8 times total. After 30 in (75 cm) (= 158 rows) total length, BO remaining 65 sts.

FRONT

Work the same as the Back, but with deeper neckline. For this, after 26½ in (67 cm) (= 142 rows) total length, BO middle 19 sts and continue both sides separately. For neckline shaping, on both sides, in every other row, BO 4 sts once, 3 sts once, 2 sts 3 times, and 1 st twice. After 30 in (75 cm) (= 158 rows) total length, BO remaining 8 sts each.

FINISHING

Close shoulder seams. With short circular needle and A, pick up and knit 104 sts around the neckline, starting in the middle of the front neckline. Join into round and work 26 rnds in Ribbing patt. In the next rnd, BO the first st and continue in back-and-forth rows with turning. After 30 rows, BO all sts.

For the left side edging, using a long circular needle and A, pick up and knit 217 sts from the bottom edge of the back over the shoulder to the bottom edge of the front, then work 1 WS row as follows: *k1, p1, rep from * to last st, k1. After this, work 2 rows in Double Seed st. In Rnd 3, make 3 buttonholes as follows: 156 sts in Double Seed st, *BO 2 sts, 18 sts in Double Seed st, repeat from * once, BO 2 sts, 16 sts in Double Seed st. In the next WS row, CO new sts over the bound-off sts of the previous row and integrate new sts into Double Seed st patt. Work another 2 rows in Double Seed st, then BO all sts.

Work right side edging mirror-inverted.

Hide all ends. Attach buttons to inside of side edges to correspond with buttonhole placement.

Soak pieces in lukewarm water, carefully press out excess water, and place on a soft surface for blocking.

KNITTING BASICS

Basic Long-Tail Cast-On

The basic long-tail cast-on produces a cast-on edge of medium elasticity.

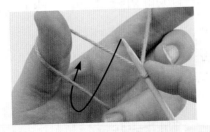

Make a slipknot and place it on a needle; press the slipknot to the working needle with the index finger of your right hand. Spread thumb and index finger of your left hand. Lead the yarn tail over the thumb and the working yarn over the index finger, grasping them with the free fingers of your left hand to pull them taut.

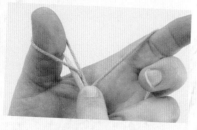

Lift the thumb and pull the working needle downwards in front of the thumb until the thumb strands cross each other in the front (thumb cross). Pass the tip of the needle below the outermost thumb strand, and lead it from right to left behind the index finger strand in the direction of the arrow as shown.

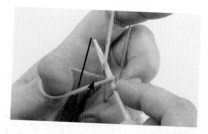

Grasp the index finger strand with the needle, and pull it through the thumb loop in the direction of the arrow. Let the loop slip from the thumb and pull the yarn tail with the thumb until a stitch has formed on the working needle. Lift the thumb, and lower the needle. Repeat the steps until the desired number of stitches has been cast on.

The first and all following odd-numbered rows are often worked as wrong-side rows. This should be kept in mind when working from a pattern where the first row mentioned is a right-side row!

A different, but also very pretty, cast-on edge can be created by working the first row and all odd-numbered rows as right-side rows.

TIP
If working the long-tail cast-on with a larger needle size or with 2 needles held together, the stitches of the first row will appear larger than those of the other rows in the knitted piece later on.

Provisional Cast-On from a Crocheted Chain

For this fast and easy-to-work cast-on method, first, using a piece of waste yarn, loosely crochet a chain of about 10 chains more than the number of stitches needed to be cast on.

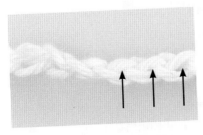

Loosely knot the end of the crocheted chain to temporarily secure. On the back of the crocheted chain, the horizontal bumps of individual chains are visible.

When it's time to undo the crocheted cast-on, pull out the loose beginning knot, and carefully unravel the chain, transferring live stitches to your knitting needle as they become freed, only continuing to unravel the chain after open stitches have been secured.

Using the project yarn, pick up and knit stitches from this chain. Make sure not to accidentally pierce the waste yarn, which would make pulling out the chain later impossible.

HINT
You will pick up 1 stitch fewer than originally cast on. Additionally, loops will appear shifted by half a stitch, so that at both edges half a stitch each will get "lost."

TIP
A crochet hook several sizes larger than normally recommended for the yarn used will make the work much easier.

Make 1 Increase from the Bar between Stitches (M1)

If the bar lifted between stitches is worked off as is, a small hole will be visible between stitches, and the increase will not appear slanted.

For a make 1 increase from the bar between stitches, insert the left needle from front to back under the bar between stitches, between the stitch worked last and the following stitch to be worked next. Lift the bar between stitches onto the left needle. It should sit on the needle with the same orientation as all other stitches.

For a knit increase, now knit the lifted bar.

For a purl increase, now purl the lifted bar.

The stitches in the newly created column over the little hole will have no slant. If a purl increase is worked in a wrong side row, it will later on the right side look the same as a regular knit increase worked in a right side row.

If make 1 increases from the bar between stitches before and after a column of one or more stitches are stacked atop each other, little eyelets will accentuate the symmetrical increase. The overall stitch direction will become slanted on account of the added stitches.

Make 1 Increase from the Bar between Stitches Worked through the Back Loop (M1L/M1R)

Increases from the bar between stitches that are worked through the back loop will look left- or right-slanted in the knitted fabric, depending on whether the bar between stitches has been lifted onto the left needle as is or twisted.

LEFT-SLANTING INCREASE KNITTED THROUGH THE BACK LOOP (M1L)

With the left needle, lift the bar between stitches from front to back.

To knit through the back loop, insert the right needle from right to left below the back leg of the stitch, grasp the working yarn, pull it through, and lift the loop from the left needle.

RIGHT-SLANTING INCREASE KNITTED THROUGH THE BACK LOOP (M1R)

Insert the left needle from back to front below the bar between stitches and lift the bar onto the needle twisted.

Insert the right needle from left to right below the front leg of the stitch, grasp the working yarn, pull it through, and lift the loop from the left needle.

Bobble from One Stitch

To make a bobble, you work several stitches into one stitch, in place of which the bobble will appear. You will alternate k1, p1 into the same stitch, but leaving the stitch on the needle.

Hold the working yarn behind the work. Insert the right needle from front to back below the front leg of the stitch and knit this stitch.

Bring the working yarn to the front, insert the needle from back to front below the front leg of the stitch, and purl this stitch.

Repeat Steps 1 and 2 until the desired width for the bobble has been reached. The initial stitch will be significantly widened by this.

For the smallest bobble, without further intermittent rows, now pass all stitches one by one over the last stitch on the right needle as well as over the needle tip, and let them slip from the left needle.

In addition to over how many stitches widthwise a bobble is worked, its size can be modified by adding a few intermittent short rows, which will be worked over the bobble stitches only. For this, turn work and work back on the wrong side over the bobble stitches only, turn work again and work on the right side over these stitches. After this, pass the bobble stitches one by one over the last stitch on the right needle.

When working the first stitch after the bobble, pull the stitch wide when inserting the needle so that the stitch below the bobble will constrict again.

TIP
By working more rows in between, the bobble can be made even larger.

Binding Off (Standard)

When binding off by passing over, you always work over two stitches. The first stitch will then be passed over the second stitch and the tip of the needle so that the top of the stitch will drape like a noose around the legs of the stitch on the needle.

BINDING OFF KNITWISE

Binding off knitwise is the easiest and most common way to bind off stitches. Worked in a right-side row, the bind-off edge will blend in with Stockinette fabric. To prevent the bind-off edge from pulling in, work the bind-off row loosely if possible. It might be helpful to use a larger needle size for this. With regular working yarn tension, you will get a bind-off edge of medium elasticity.

At the beginning of the bind-off row, knit 2 stitches. Insert the left needle from left to right into the front leg of the right stitch, pass it over the left stitch and over the tip of the needle, and let it slip off the needle. Do not further tighten the working yarn.

*Knit another stitch, again pass the right one of the two stitches over the left stitch and the needle tip, and let it slip off the left-hand needle.

Repeat the working steps from *.

BINDING OFF IN PATTERN

When combining binding off in knit and purl, it is also possible to bind off in stitch pattern. For this, stitches have to be worked in the stitch pattern used prior to binding them off. Lace patterns are best bound off in purl in a wrong-side row. Increases and decreases may also be incorporated into the bind-off edge before stitches are passed over. If possible, yarn overs and bobbles as well as all decorative elements that gather stitches together should be skipped when the bind-off edge will later be seamed since they would add unnecessary bulk to a seam.

When binding off cables, the edge will often turn out wider than the part worked in cable pattern. Cables pull in the knitted fabric, so when no more cables are crossed in the bind-off row, the fabric expands and does not match the rest of the knitted piece (see above right in photo). If, however, while binding off, depending on the cable, 1 to 3 stitches are decreased, the width of the bind-off row will again match the width of the knitted piece (at left above). How many stitches to decrease depends on the width of the cable: For cables over 4 stitches, reducing by 1 stitch will be sufficient; for cables over 6 stitches and more, 2 stitches should be reduced.

Grafting in Kitchener Stitch

With Kitchener stitch, rows of live stitches can be grafted so that the yarn from the grafting row will blend in as just another row of the knitted fabric. Kitchener stitch is used where a regular seamed edge would feel uncomfortable when the garment is being worn, or when a seam of the same elasticity as the knitted fabric is desired.

TIP
Whether you insert the needle knitwise or purlwise will determine whether the stitch formed with the grafting strand will look like a knit or purl stitch.

Place both pieces to be seamed flat on the table, both with right sides facing you. Both rows of live stitches are still on their needles. The needles are placed next to each other with both needle tips pointing to the right.

Thread the grafting thread into a tapestry needle. Insert the tapestry needle into the selvedge stitch on the front needle purlwise, and pull the grafting thread through to the last 6 in (15 cm) to be used later for securing. Insert the tapestry needle knitwise into the selvedge stitch of the top needle and pull the yarn through. Both stitches still remain on the needle.

From this position, hold both knitting needles with your left hand. Needles are aligned parallel. Wrong sides of both knitted pieces face each other.

You will now alternate working 2 stitches from the front and 2 stitches from the back needle, as follows (for Stockinette st fabric):

1. Thread yarn through first stitch on front needle as if to knit. Slip stitch off needle.
2. Thread yarn through next stitch on front needle as if to purl. Leave stitch on needle.
3. Thread yarn through first stitch on back needle as if to purl. Slip stitch off needle.
4. Thread yarn through next stitch on back needle as if to knit. Leave stitch on needle.
Repeat these 4 steps.

Mattress Stitch

Seaming in mattress stitch is the most commonly used method for joining two knitted pieces. It is worked on the right side of the fabric, where the seam is visible at all times and can be adjusted to the pattern, allowing it to create a nearly invisible seam.

Mattress stitch can be used to seam all edges with closed stitches from cast-on or bind-off edges, as well as columns of selvedge stitches at the side edges of knitted pieces. Selvedge stitches or the top row will fold inwards, resulting in a bulky seam. This seam turns out less elastic than the knitted fabric.

With a carefully sewn mattress stitch seam, all edges with closed stitches from cast-on or bind-off rows and all side edges can be joined so the seam blends in with the stitch pattern. If two pieces need to be joined where stitch columns meet stitch rows, the difference between stitch height and width needs to be accounted for and adjusted. Along vertical edges, depending on the stitch pattern, either 1 or 2 bars between stitches need to be picked up, while on horizontal ones along cast-on or bind-off rows, the seam is always worked over both legs of the same stitch. This means that independently of the stitch pattern, the tapestry needle will always grasp 2 strands—in this case not bars between stitches, but legs of the same stitch.

JOINING 2 SIDE EDGES

When seaming 2 side edges, 2 columns of stitches of equal height meet. In addition to the required cast-on number, 1 more selvedge stitch for each edge has to be worked as seam allowance for both knitted pieces. The selvedge stitches of both pieces will fold inwards after seaming.

Place the two pieces to be joined next to each other right side up so their edges meet. Join the selvedge sts from the bottom (cast-on) edge of both pieces in a figure-8 motion by going through both pieces, inserting the tapestry needle directly above the cast-on edge from the back to the front and from the bottom up, exiting before the selvedge stitch of the left piece, from the bottom up, exiting before the selvedge stitch of the right piece, then pulling the yarn through. Leave an end of at least 6 in (15 cm) to weave in later.

Exit a second time in the same spot, again from the bottom up, first on the left piece, then on the right piece, then tighten the yarn properly.

COLORWORK AND PATTERN CHARTS

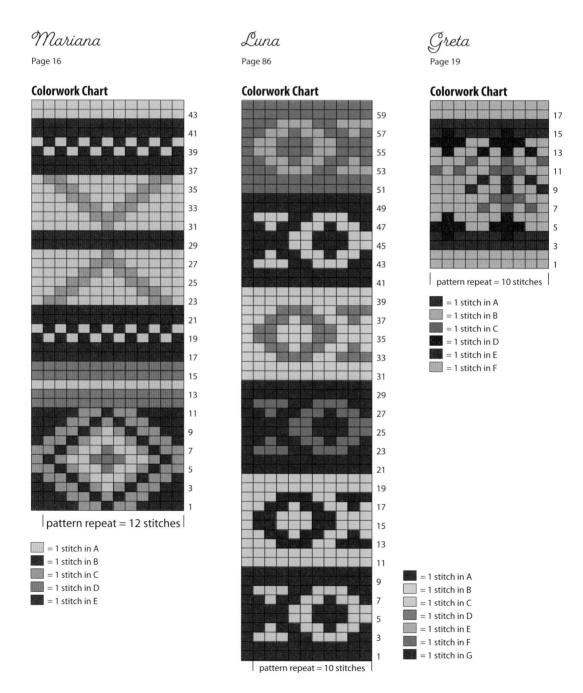

Mariana

Page 16

Colorwork Chart

pattern repeat = 12 stitches

☐ = 1 stitch in A
■ = 1 stitch in B
☐ = 1 stitch in C
▨ = 1 stitch in D
■ = 1 stitch in E

Luna

Page 86

Colorwork Chart

pattern repeat = 10 stitches

■ = 1 stitch in A
☐ = 1 stitch in B
☐ = 1 stitch in C
▨ = 1 stitch in D
▨ = 1 stitch in E
▨ = 1 stitch in F
■ = 1 stitch in G

Greta

Page 19

Colorwork Chart

pattern repeat = 10 stitches

■ = 1 stitch in A
☐ = 1 stitch in B
▨ = 1 stitch in C
■ = 1 stitch in D
■ = 1 stitch in E
☐ = 1 stitch in F

Smilla

Page 89

Colorwork Chart A

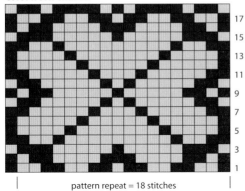

17
15
13
11
9
7
5
3
1

pattern repeat = 18 stitches

Colorwork Chart B

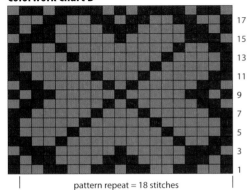

17
15
13
11
9
7
5
3
1

pattern repeat = 18 stitches

Colorwork Chart C

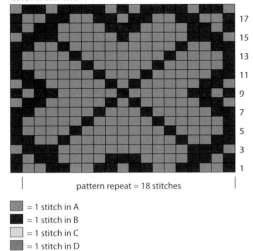

17
15
13
11
9
7
5
3
1

pattern repeat = 18 stitches

☐ = 1 stitch in A
■ = 1 stitch in B
☐ = 1 stitch in C
☐ = 1 stitch in D

Nadia

Page 83

Colorwork Chart

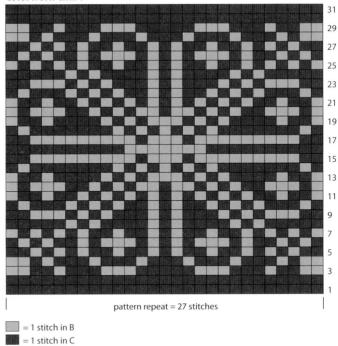

31
29
27
25
23
21
19
17
15
13
11
9
7
5
3
1

pattern repeat = 27 stitches

☐ = 1 stitch in B
■ = 1 stitch in C

Melina

Page 51

Colorwork Chart

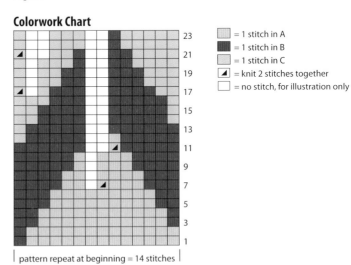

23
21
19
17
15
13
11
9
7
5
3
1

pattern repeat at beginning = 14 stitches

☐ = 1 stitch in A
■ = 1 stitch in B
☐ = 1 stitch in C
◣ = knit 2 stitches together
☐ = no stitch, for illustration only

103

Mila

Page 38

Chart

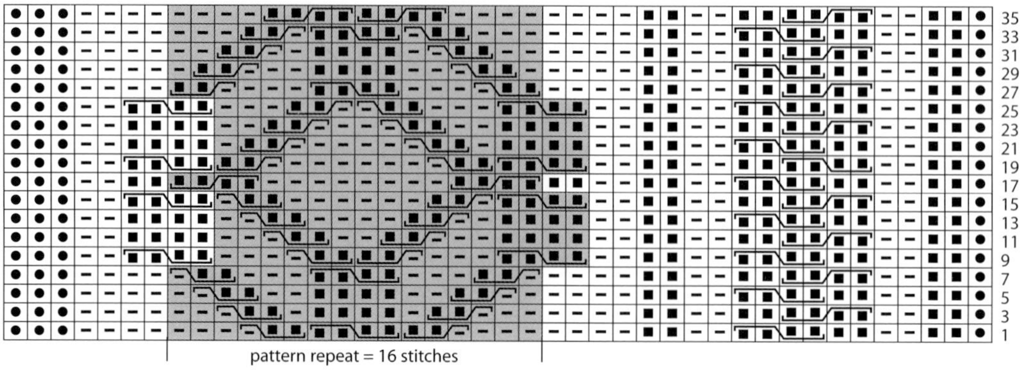

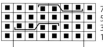

35
33
31
29
27
25
23
21
19
17
15
13
11
9
7
5
3
1

pattern repeat = 16 stitches

⬤ = 1 selvedge stitch

■ = knit 1 stitch

— = purl 1 stitch

= hold 1 stitch on cable needle behind work, knit 2 stitches, then purl 1 stitch from cable needle

= hold 2 stitches on cable needle in front of work, purl 1 stitch, then knit 2 stitches from cable needle

= hold 2 stitches on cable needle behind work, knit 2 stitches, then knit 2 stitches from cable needle

= hold 2 stitches on cable needle in front of work, knit 2 stitches, then knit 2 stitches from cable needle

---

Helena

Page 68

Chart A

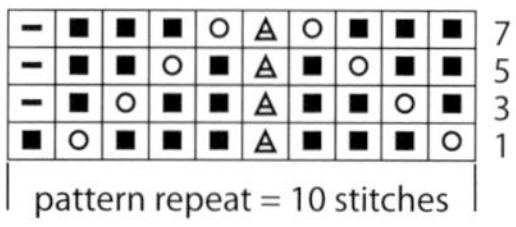

7
5
3
1

pattern repeat = 10 stitches

Chart B

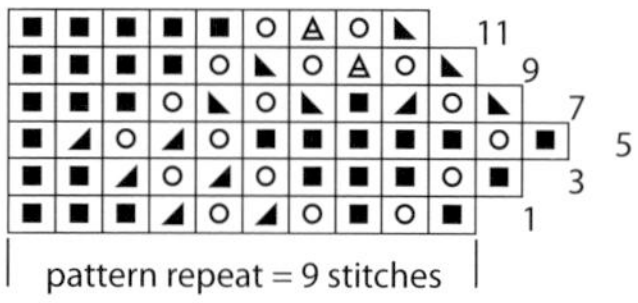

11
9
7
5
3
1

pattern repeat = 9 stitches

■ = knit 1 stitch

— = purl 1 stitch

○ = make 1 yarn over

▲ = sk2p: slip 1 stitch knitwise, knit 2 stitches together, pass the slipped stitch over

◢ = knit 2 stitches together

◣ = skp: slip 1 stitch knitwise, knit the next stitch, pass the slipped stitch over

---

Smilla

Page 89

Chart 1

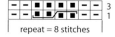

3
1

repeat = 8 stitches

Chart 2

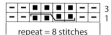

3
1

repeat = 8 stitches

■ = knit 1 stitch

— = purl 1 stitch

= hold 2 stitches on cable needle behind work, knit 2 stitches, then knit 2 stitches from cable needle

= hold 2 stitches on cable needle in front of work, knit 2 stitches, then knit 2 stitches from cable needle

---

Nadia

Page 83

Chart

7
5
3
1

pattern repeat = 6 stitches

■ = knit 1 stitch

= hold 2 stitches on cable needle behind work, knit 2 stitches, then knit 2 stitches from cable needle

= hold 2 stitches on cable needle in front of work, knit 2 stitches, then knit 2 stitches from cable needle

Page 30

Chart A

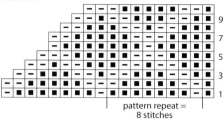

pattern repeat = 8 stitches

In order to better show the stitch pattern, charts show right side and wrong side rows as viewed from the right side of the knitted fabric. Accordingly, stitches shown as "knit" are to be purled in wrong-side rows, and stitches shown as

Chart B

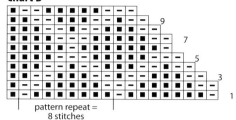

pattern repeat = 8 stitches

"purl" are to be knitted in wrong-side rows (please also refer to knitting symbol legend).

■ = RS: knit 1 stitch; WS: purl 1 stitch
− = RS: purl 1 stitch; WS: knit 1 stitch

Nora

Page 33

Cable Pattern, Chart A

pattern repeat = 32 stitches

■ = knit 1 stitch

− = purl 1 stitch

ɔ| = slip 1 stitch purlwise with yarn behind work

= hold 1 stitch on cable needle in front of work, purl 1 stitch, then knit 1 stitch from cable needle

= hold 1 stitch on cable needle behind work, knit 1 stitch, then purl 1 stitch from cable needle

= hold 1 stitch on cable needle in front of work, knit 1 stitch, then knit 1 stitch from cable needle

= hold 1 stitch on cable needle behind work, knit 1 stitch, then knit 1 stitch from cable needle

Bias Stripe Pattern, Chart B

pattern repeat = 8 stitches

= hold 1 stitch on cable needle behind work, knit 2 stitches, then purl 1 stitch from cable needle

= hold 2 stitches on cable needle in front of work, purl 1 stitch, then knit 2 stitches from cable needle

= hold 2 stitches on cable needle behind work, knit 2 stitches, then knit 2 stitches from cable needle

Finja

Page 27

Chart

pattern repeat = 24 stitches

ɔ| = slip 1 stitch purlwise with yarn behind work

− = purl 1 stitch

= hold 1 stitch on cable needle behind work, knit 2 stitches, then purl 1 stitch from cable needle

= hold 2 stitches on cable needle in front of work, purl 1 stitch, then knit 2 stitches from cable needle

Fiona

Page 48

Chart

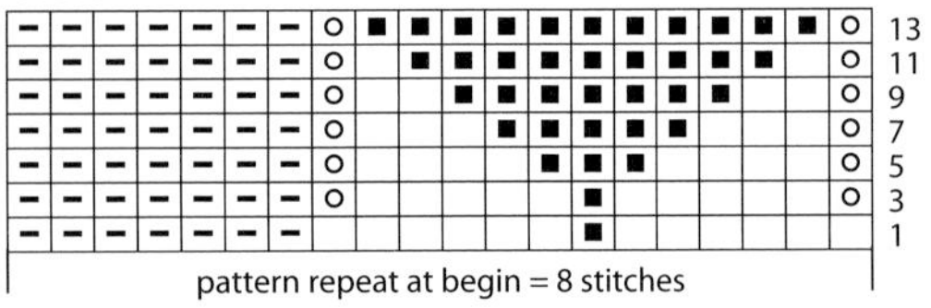

pattern repeat at begin = 8 stitches

13 11 9 7 5 3 1

 = knit 1 stitch

 = purl 1 stitch

 = make 1 yarn over

= no stitch, for illustration only

Lissi

Page 76

Chart A

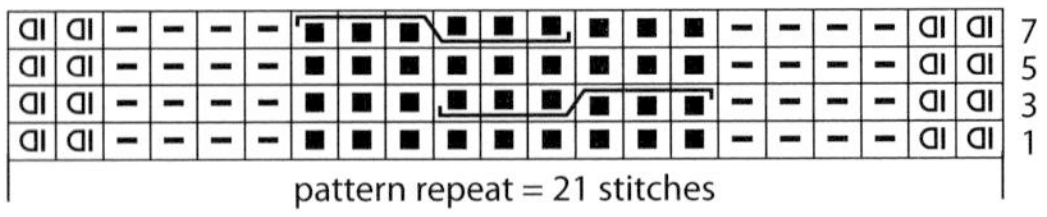

pattern repeat = 21 stitches

7 5 3 1

Chart B

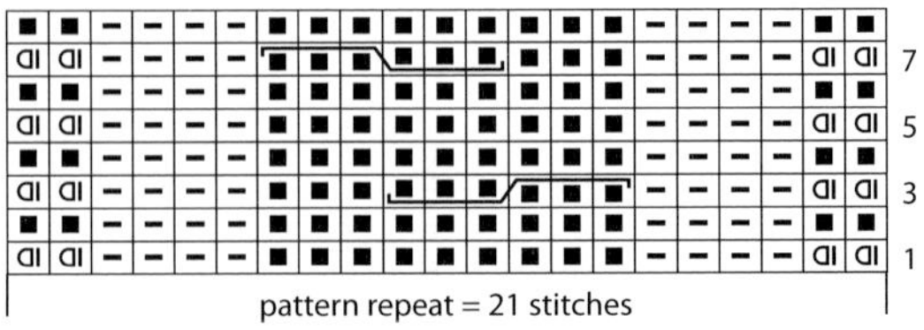

pattern repeat = 21 stitches

7 5 3 1

= slip 1 stitch purlwise with yarn behind work

= knit 1 stitch

= purl 1 stitch

= hold 3 stitches on cable needle behind work, knit 3, then knit 3 stitches from cable needle

= hold 3 stitches on cable needle in front of work, knit 3, then knit 3 stitches from cable needle

Celina

Page 58

Chart A

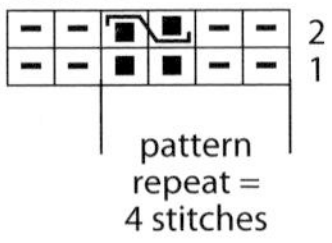

pattern repeat = 4 stitches

2 1

Chart B

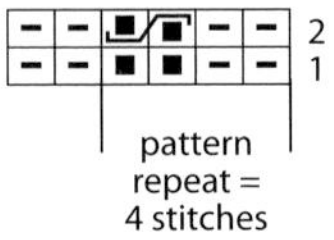

pattern repeat = 4 stitches

2 1

Chart C

pattern repeat = 36 stitches

15 13 11 9 7 5 3 1

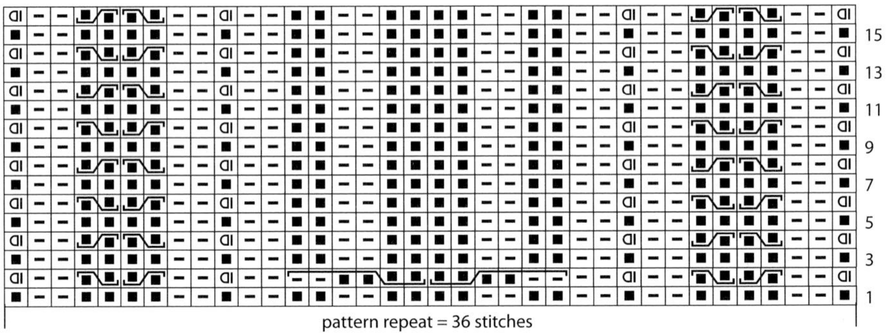

= purl 1 stitch

= knit 1 stitch

= slip 1 stitch purlwise with yarn behind work

= hold 1 stitch on cable needle in front of work, knit 1 stitch, then knit 1 stitch from cable needle

= hold 1 stitch on cable needle behind work, knit 1 stitch, then knit 1 stitch from cable needle

= hold 2 stitches on cable needle in front of work, knit 2 stitches, and purl 2 stitches, then knit 2 stitches from cable needle

= hold 4 stitches on cable needle behind work, knit 2 stitches, then purl 2 stitches and knit 2 stitches from cable needle

Jaina

Chart A

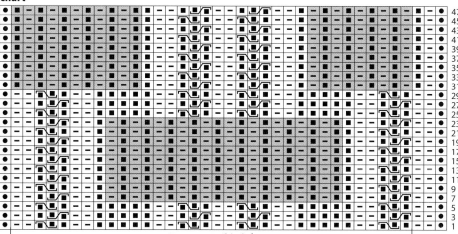

pattern repeat = 10 stitches

Chart B

pattern repeat = 16 stitches

■ = knit 1 stitch

− = purl 1 stitch

O = make 1 yarn over

◢ = knit 2 stitches together

◣ = skp: slip 1 stitch knitwise, knit the next stitch, pass the slipped stitch over

▲ = sk2p: slip 1 stitch knitwise, knit 2 stitches together, pass the slipped stitch over

= hold 2 stitches on cable needle in front of work, knit 2 stitches, then knit 2 stitches from cable needle

= hold 2 stitches on cable needle behind work, knit 2 stitches, then knit 2 stitches from cable needle

= hold 2 stitches on cable needle in front of work, purl 2 stitches, then knit 2 stitches from cable needle

= hold 2 stitches on cable needle behind work, knit 2 stitches, then purl 2 stitches from cable needle

Ophelia

Chart

pattern repeat = 34 stitches

Only right side rows are shown; in wrong side rows, work back across row just worked, working the stitches as stated in knitting symbol legend; purl all cable stitches.

● = 1 selvedge stitch (RS: knit 1 stitch; WS: purl 1 stitch)

■ = RS: knit 1 stitch; WS: purl 1 stitch

− = RS: purl 1 stitch; WS: knit 1 stitch

▨ = RS and WS: knit 1 stitch

▭ = RS and WS: purl 1 stitch

= hold 1 stitch on cable needle in front of work, knit 1 stitch, then knit 1 stitch from cable needle

= hold 1 stitch on cable needle behind work, knit 1 stitch, then knit 1 stitch from cable needle

107

Ilka

Page 71

Chart A

	23
	21
	19
	17
	15
	13
	11
	9
	7
	5
	3
	1

pattern repeat = 8 stitches

Chart B

	23
	21
	19
	17
	15
	13
	11
	9
	7
	5
	3
	1

pattern repeat = 8 stitches

■ = 1 knit 1 stitch

+ = make 1 knit stitch from the bar between stitches

✖ = skp: slip 1 stitch knitwise, knit the next stitch, pass the slipped stitch over

◢ = knit 2 stitches together

◣ = skp: slip 1 stitch knitwise, knit the next stitch, pass the slipped stitch over

Ava

Page 56

Chart A

pattern repeat = 18 stitches

○ = make 1 yarn over

◣ = skp: slip 1 stitch knitwise, knit the next stitch, pass the slipped stitch over

◢ = knit 2 stitches together

△ = sk2p: slip 1 stitch knitwise, knit 2 stitches together, pass the slipped stitch over

□ = no stitch, for illustration only

Chart B

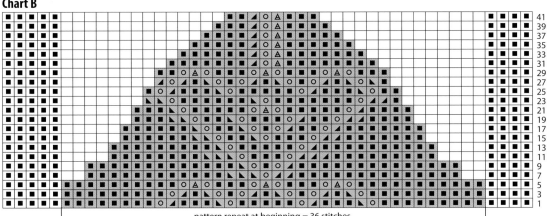

pattern repeat at beginning = 36 stitches

108

ABBREVIATIONS

approx = approximately

BO = bind off

ch = chain

cn = cable needle

CO = cast on

DPN(s) = double pointed needle(s)

k = knit

k2tog = knit 2 stitches together

k3tog = knit 3 stitches together

M1L = make 1 left: With the left needle, lift the bar between the stitch last worked and the stitch to be worked next from front to back, and knit this stitch through the back loop.

M1R = make 1 right: With the left needle, lift the bar between the stitch last worked and the stitch to be worked next from back to front and knit this stitch.

p = purl

p2tog = purl 2 stitches together

patt = pattern

pm = place marker

rep = repeat

rnd(s) = round(s)

RS = right side (row)

sc = single crochet

selv st(s) = selvedge stitch(es)

sk2p = slip 1 stitch knitwise, knit 2 stitches together, pass the slipped stitch over

skp = slip 1 stitch knitwise, knit the next stitch, pass the slipped stitch over

sl = slip stitch without working it

sm = slip marker

st(s) = stitch(es)

tbl = through back loop

WS = wrong side (row)

yo('s) = yarn over(s)

ACKNOWLEDGMENTS

How might one picture the work to write a book containing 30 poncho and cape designs? A rather solitary pursuit, you might envision. Making yarn selections, thinking up designs, swatching, and writing pattern instructions all require lots of time and focus. Finally, samples have to be knit up as well. How can this be done on one's own? I can't imagine how other designers manage. I, for one, need a first-class knitting team to support my endeavors, and thankfully I have found it. Together, we knitted, cursed, corrected, unraveled, and knitted again until all samples looked as they were supposed to.

For this reason, my very special thanks go out to the world's best knitting team—without you, this book would not have turned out the way it has:

Helga Dorn (Vivien)
Andrea Eisenbarth (Ophelia)
Christine Gahbler (Jaina)
Stephanie Häuslmann (Nora)
Sabine Hardtke (Fiona and Nadia)
Michaela Herweg (Finja and Luna)
Michael Hinz (Leana, Fria, and Maja)
Viola Keller (Mariana)
Katharina Klusmann (Celina)
Heike Kuhn (Ava)
Mareike Lachmann (Melina)
Paula Lauter (Rabea)
Monica Lauenstein (Romy)
Marion-Anett Sewing (Alida)
Mandy Theinert (Helena)
Britta Türke (Ilka)
Yvonne Weber (Ronja)

ABOUT THE AUTHOR

For Rita Maassen, designing is a passion. The web and graphic designer has been enthralled with knitting since childhood. Very early on, she became enthusiastic about creating her own designs, and ever since then, she has been creating new knitting designs in her small studio in Germany's Lower Rhine region. Since 2010, she has been offering her handmade fashion and numerous knitting patterns under her own Fashionworks label. Her work has been published in a variety of print magazines and online editions, and her Facebook page and blog are enjoying a steadily growing fan base as well.

THANK YOU

We would like to thank companies MEZ GmbH (Kenzingen), www.mezcrafts.com; Lang & Co. AG (Reiden), www.langyarns.com; and Hohenloher Wolle GmbH (Wallhausen), www.schoppel-wolle .com; and www.schachenmayr.com for their support with this book.